THE BAFFLED PARENT'S
GUIDE TO
GREAT BASKETBALL
PLAYS

Coach Fran Dunphy and
Lawrence Hsieh

Mc Graw Hill

Camden, Maine • New York • Chicago • San Francisco
Lisbon • London • Madrid • Mexico City • Milan • New Delhi
San Juan • Seoul • Singapore • Sydney • Toronto

*To my all-star team: my wife, Janice, and my children, Jennifer and Jason,
who inspire and amaze me every day; and to my parents, Mary and
Dr. J. S. Hsieh, who taught me well.*
—Lawrence Hsieh

The **McGraw·Hill** Companies

1 2 3 4 5 6 7 8 9   DOC DOC   3 2 1 0 9

*Library of Congress Cataloging-in-Publication Data may be obtained from the Library of
Congress.*

ISBN 978-0-07-150279-5
MHID 0-07-150279-3

Questions regarding the content of this book should be addressed to
www.internationalmarine.com

Questions regarding the ordering of this book should be addressed to
The McGraw-Hill Companies
Customer Service Department
P.O. Box 547
Blacklick, OH 43004
Retail customers: 1-800-262-4729
Bookstores: 1-800-722-4726

Unless otherwise noted, all photographs by Shelley Cryan Photography, LLC.

Contents

Part One   The Playbook

Part Two   The Fundamentals

Introduction

So you're a Baffled Parent.

You introduced your child to the exciting and fast-paced game of basketball. You're ecstatic because he or she loves it and has signed up for league play. But instead of just dropping him off at practices and cheering at games, you've signed yourself up too. Or perhaps it would be more accurate to say that you've been drafted. The league asked for volunteer coaches, and you couldn't find a graceful way to say no.

Now you're looking at the ten or twelve young faces of your team— eager, bored, restless, enthusiastic, nervous, expectant—and you're wondering what you've gotten yourself into. These kids need a mentor, a teacher, a motivator, a strategist. They need a coach. You're not a coach, you're a parent who knows little or nothing about organized basketball. How do you even begin?

Don't panic. You can do this.

As a youth basketball coach, your job will be to teach your players the game's fundamental skills—physical and mental—in a safe and fun environment. A good basketball player should know how to shoot, dribble, and pass the ball properly—that much is fairly obvious. But he or she should also know the ins and outs of tactics, floor spacing, movement, and team play on offense and defense. He needs court awareness. She should know when to shoot the ball, when to pass, when to drive to the basket, and when and where to move without the ball. He should not be afraid to take an open shot, but he should also know when a shot is not the best option.

The popular youth sports differ widely in their character. For example, soccer is a highly improvisational sport, while success in football relies on a variety of set plays used to advance the ball down the field and create scoring opportunities, with the game stopping after each play is run. Basketball is unique in its combination of improvisation with choreographed plays. It offers a wonderful blend of pattern and structure embedded within continuous flow and movement. It's a great sport, and you're going to have a great experience as a coach. We guarantee it.

This is the only book to show you how to teach game-winning basketball plays to players up to 14 years old (through middle school and junior high school) within the context of the game's fundamentals. We'll give you the X's and O's in their proper coaching context.

How to Use This Book

This book has two parts. Part One, The Playbook, contains 50 basic to intermediate plays plus 28 variations (what we call second options). Part Two, The Fundamentals, offers an overview of the skills and concepts your players will need in order to execute the plays and to defend against them.

In basketball there are continuity plays, set plays, and plays for special situations. A young team needs no more than one to four plays from each of those categories—much more than that is probably overkill, especially early in the season. The reason we offer such a great variety of plays in the Playbook is so that you can pick the few that work best for your team, your players, and your coaching style.

Chapter 1 presents continuity plays, each of which is a choreographed sequence of player movements involving all five players. Unlike a set play, which has a defined end point, a continuity play is a repeating pattern that goes on until it is interrupted by a scoring opportunity (or a turnover!).

Begin your season by teaching one or two continuity plays from Chapter 1, because these establish your offensive sets and patterns. They teach your kids how to space themselves on the floor, how to move without the ball, how to set screens, and how to dribble with purpose. They involve all the players, so that all of them—not just the ones with the most advanced skills—feel like important parts of the team. One good continuity play will transform your offense from chaos to a machine. And continuity plays provide the context within which the game's skills—passing, dribbling, shooting, moving, rebounding—can be practiced and refined.

One continuity play to use against a man-to-man defense and one to use against a zone defense are probably all you need.

Chapters 2 through 8 present a variety of set plays. Think of a set play not as an alternative to your continuity offense but as something embedded within or erected atop it. A set play is designed to create a scoring opportunity for one or two of your players against weak points in the defense. Start the season with one set play. Add another when your players are ready for it. Maybe you can add a third or even a fourth by the end of the season, but not if it makes things overly complicated. Keep things simple.

Chapters 9 and 10 give you plays for special situations: a fast break; beating a full-court press; and inbounding the ball from the sideline or the baseline. Your team needs an adequate response for each such situation, and we give you several options to choose from. Pick the ones that you think will provide the best fit for your players, and as the season progresses and the need arises, don't be afraid to try something else.

Each play in this book is presented with a diagram and a step-by-step description of its execution. We show you how the play leads to scoring opportunities and which fundamental skills and concepts the play emphasizes. And we show how the play can be defended—not only so that your players know what to expect on offense, but also so that they become better defenders. Offense and defense are two sides of the same coin in basketball, and this book will help you coach both.

Many of the plays include steps that incorporate terms (down screen, etc.) that are defined in the glossary and described in greater detail in Part Two, The Fundamentals. In writing the book, we've envisioned that you'll flip back and forth as needed among the Playbook, the Fundamentals, and the glossary.

Finally, in basketball, as in life, even the best-laid plans often fail or need adjustment on the fly in the face of a tough and well-prepared defense. Thus, most plays include a selection of second options for the offense to try when the first option becomes unavailable or the play breaks down.

Part Two, The Fundamentals, will help you teach your young players the basics of playing defense, making individual offensive moves, passing, rebounding, setting screens, and shooting the ball. Because this book functions primarily as a playbook, we do not cover these skills and concepts in as much depth as you can find in a basketball instructional manual. If you need more on the fundamentals, check out the other Baffled Parent's Guides listed on page 5. But we believe that this book's presentation of the fundamentals in the context of the plays themselves is uniquely useful, making this book a good adjunct to any other basketball coaching manual as well as a stand-alone guide for a successful season.

Any basketball play is the sum of its parts. Your team can't execute a pass-and-screen-away play effectively if the players don't know how to set an effective screen, how to use the screen properly to get free, how to pass the ball to the freed player, how to catch the ball, and how to make a layup. On defense, the players will have to know how to defend the player with the ball and the players away from the ball. They'll need to know how to defend against plays designed to cause defensive confusion, exploit weak links, and create mismatches. The Fundamentals section is here to show you how to teach your players the components of a wide range of offensive and defensive skills, so that with repetition and practice your players will be able to mix and match the skills to execute good plays and defend against any situation.

A Word on Coaching

There's a fine line in youth sports between teaching your athletes how to play versus drilling them on what to do. This is not a book of plays to be memorized and executed in rote fashion. Rather, instill in your players that the plays you teach them (and which will form the building blocks of the more advanced plays they'll learn in high school and perhaps beyond) are merely a means to an end—tools designed to create scoring opportunities by manufacturing and exploiting defensive gaps and lapses. A scoring opportunity may arise anywhere in the middle of a play, not just at its end. Good coaches (and for that matter good teachers, bosses, and parents) give their charges the tools to succeed but encourage them to think freely and make decisions without inhibition. If a player is able to exploit a sudden scoring opportunity or even create one himself without being a selfish teammate, he or she should not be penalized for tweaking the play in order to do it.

You are going to have a terrifc season. One or two continuity plays and one or two set plays will give you all the structure you need to teach your players the game. Add a fast-break play, a way to beat a press, and a couple of inbounding plays and you've got the building blocks of a successful season. And more important, you'll be giving your players the introduction to the game they need to play basketball through high school or beyond.

Most kids are eager learners. It's amazing to see what they can learn and master in just one season. Good luck in all you do, and have a great season!

The authors (Lawrence Hsieh, back row, left, and Fran Dunphy, back row, fourth from left) with their demonstration basketball players and coaches.

Look for these other Baffled Parent's Guides

Coaching Youth Baseball
by Bill Thurston

Great Baseball Drills
by Jim Garland

Coaching Girls' Basketball
by Sylvia Hatchell with Jeff Thomas

Coaching Youth Basketball
by David G. Faucher

Great Basketball Drills
by Jim Garland

Coaching Youth Football
by Paul Pasqualoni with Jim McLaughlin

Youth Football Skills and Drills
by Tom Bass

Coaching Youth Hockey
by Bruce Driver with Clare Wharton

Coaching Boys' Lacrosse
by Greg Murrell and Jim Garland

Coaching Girls' Lacrosse
by Janine Tucker and Maryalice Yakutchik

Coaching Girls' Soccer
by Drayson Hounsome

Coaching 6-and-Under Soccer
by David Williams and Scott Graham

Coaching Youth Soccer
by Bobby Clark

Great Soccer Drills
by Tom Fleck and Ron Quinn

Coaching Youth Softball
by Jacquie Joseph

Coaching Tee Ball
by Bing Broido

PART ONE

The Playbook

Game Basics and the Fundamentals of Offense

This chapter provides the context for the play diagrams and descriptions in the chapters that follow. We need a shared language for referring to areas of the court, player roles, and player positions in the common offensive formations. Once we have that, the play diagrams will make perfect sense and we'll minimize the opportunities for misinterpretation.

Note that at their first use, basketball terms used throughout the book are in *italic* and defined or explained. (Also see the glossary on page 125.)

About the Game

The Court

The most concrete context for the game of basketball is, of course, the *court* on which the game is played. College courts are 94 feet long and 50 feet wide, though the dimensions of youth league and middle school courts vary. But all courts include the features identified in the court diagram. The inbounds area is defined by two *sidelines* and two *baselines*. A *midcourt line* divides the court in half. The half that is the *offensive zone* or *frontcourt* for one team is the *defensive zone* or *backcourt* for the other. The team with the ball attacks the basket in its offensive zone, and the other team defends that basket. At halftime the teams switch ends.

In a successful trip "down the floor" to its offensive zone, a team either makes a *field goal* (a basket shot against defenders) or makes one or more *foul shots* or *free throws* (undefended baskets shot from the foul line). If unsuccessful, the offensive team loses possession of the ball to the defensive team by missing a field goal or foul shot and failing to get the *rebound* (a missed shot), or by committing a *turnover* (loss of possession of the ball).

Offensive-Defensive Transitions

There are several ways in which the offensive team can turn the ball over. The defensive team can steal the ball from a player dribbling the ball, snatch

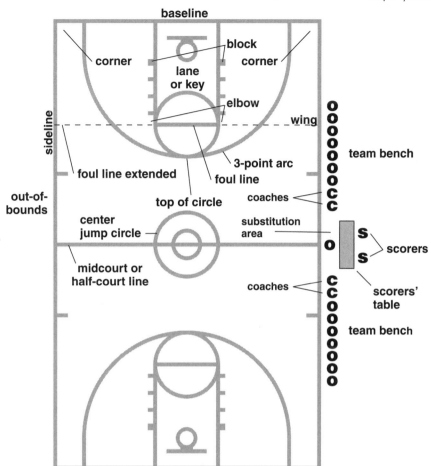

The basketball court.

a pass before the ball reaches its intended recipient, or retrieve the ball after causing the ball handler to bobble it. In any of these cases play is continuous, and the defensive team immediately becomes the new offensive team without having to inbound the ball.

The offensive team also turns the ball over if a player steps out-of-bounds while in possession of the ball, accidentally throws the ball out-of-bounds, or commits an infraction. Infractions include the closely guarded rule and other infractions discussed below, *traveling* (taking more than one step with the ball without dribbling), and committing an *offensive foul*. In any of these cases the defensive team becomes the new offensive team and either inbounds the ball from a baseline or sideline or takes a free throw, depending on the situation.

We'll discuss other turnovers where relevant. For a complete description of basketball rules, fouls, and other basics, see *The Baffled Parent's Guide to Coaching Youth Basketball* by David Faucher, and *The Baffled Parent's Guide to Coaching Girls' Basketball* by Sylvia Hatchell and Jeff Thomas.

Since the defensive team is allowed to gain possession of the ball by stealing it from a dribbler, stealing a pass, or rebounding a missed shot, the essence of successful defense is to make it hard for the other team to dribble, pass, shoot, and rebound. And the purpose of this book is to find ways around these defensive tactics.

When possession changes with a made field goal or free throw, the defensive team becomes the new offensive team, and it must inbound the ball from behind the baseline of its defensive zone and travel the length of the floor into its offensive zone.

The defensive team can also gain possession of the ball by rebounding the opponent's missed field goal or foul shot, or by stealing the ball. When possession changes in this manner, play is continuous, and the new offensive team advances the ball over the midcourt line without having to inbound. This may present a *fast-break opportunity* if the defenders are slow getting back to their defensive zone. When possession changes after an infraction, the new offensive team will either inbound the ball in its defensive zone or shoot free throws in its offensive zone, depending on the situation.

No matter how a team gains possession in its backcourt, it has 10 seconds to advance the ball over the midcourt line and into its offensive zone. Failure to get the ball into the frontcourt within 10 seconds results in a turnover. Once the offense advances the ball into the frontcourt, it may not recross the midcourt line on that trip down the floor. Inadvertently dribbling or passing the ball back over the line constitutes an *over-and-back* or *backcourt violation* — another turnover.

A Few Rules about Fouls

For our purposes in this book, we'll discuss most rules as they bear on the plays in question. Keep in mind these few rules, however, which are designed to facilitate the pace of the game and are relevant to many of the plays we'll examine:

- **Closely guarded call.** A player with the ball who is guarded by a defender within 6 feet of her must not dribble in place for longer than 5 seconds.

- **5-second call.** A player who *picks up* (gives up) his dribble must pass or shoot within 5 seconds.

- **5-second call on the inbounder.** A player inbounding the ball to a teammate must pass the ball in within 5 seconds.

- **3-second lane call.** An offensive player can't stay in the *lane* (also called the *key* or the *paint*) for longer than 3 seconds. If she steps outside the lane, she can step back in with a new 3 seconds. The count also restarts when an attempted field goal hits the rim of the basket. The rule is designed to prevent the lane area from clogging.

The Players

Each team has five players on the court, and substitutions can be made in any *dead-ball situation*—whenever the referee blows the whistle and play stops for a foul, a time-out, or the end of a quarter. You can substitute after the first of two free throws and after the last free throw but not before the first free throw, and you can't substitute for the player about to shoot a free throw.

The five players on the floor typically include two guards, two forwards, and a center (who is really a specialized forward). *Guards* are perimeter players who mainly play away from the basket on offense, but are also playmakers who create scoring opportunities by *driving* (making dribble moves) to the basket, and they guard the other team's guards on defense. *Forwards* specialize in driving to the basket or making *post-up moves* near the basket on offense. The *center* often plays with his back to the basket on offense, relying on a variety of close-range post-up moves; guards the basket on defense; and rebounds the ball at both ends of the floor.

There is much overlap in the responsibilities and desirable skill sets of these positions—more now, certainly, than there used to be. For example, the best guards are able not only to shoot the ball from the perimeter, but also to drive to the basket. Sometimes a team's best rebounder is a forward, not the center. And the best centers today are highly mobile and can play not only under the basket but 10 to 15 feet away from it. The positions often break down further like this:

- **Point Guard or 1.** The point guard is quick and the team's best ball handler. He or she dribbles the ball down the floor and directs the offense. Good offense starts with the 1 guard. The point guard often has the best *court sense* on the team, meaning that he or she is able to "see" defensive breakdowns and gaps and then think on the fly to turn these breakdowns or gaps into scoring opportunities.

- **Shooting Guard or 2.** Your 2 guard should be your best outside shooter as well as a good ball handler.

- **Small Forward or 3.** Ideally your small forward will have a good medium-range shot as well as the ability to drive to the hoop for layups and close-in shots. He or she should also be a good rebounder, though he is usually the smaller of your two forwards.

- **Power Forward or 4.** You want a good inside scorer and rebounder at this position. Your power forward is more likely to play on the post, whereas your small forward is more likely to play on the *wing*.

- **Center or 5.** This is usually your tallest player, an aggressive rebounder and an aggressive, effective defender *down low* (near the basket), where he or she blocks shots or forces the shooters to pass back to the outside or alter their shots. On offense your center plays a post position at the edge

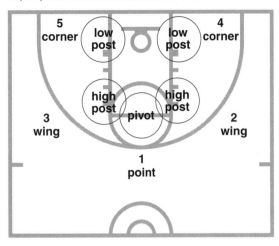

Player positions based on court location.

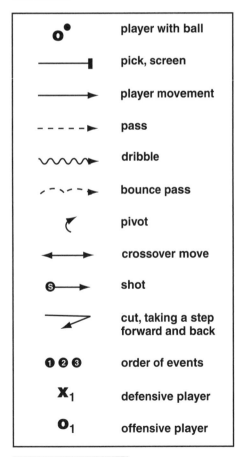

o•	player with ball
——————▌	pick, screen
——————▶	player movement
- - - - -▶	pass
∿∿∿▶	dribble
⌒⌐⌐▶	bounce pass
↶	pivot
◀——————▶	crossover move
Ⓢ——▶	shot
⟋⟍	cut, taking a step forward and back
❶ ❷ ❸	order of events
X_1	defensive player
O_1	offensive player

Diagram key.

of the lane—either a *low post position* on one of the blocks or a *high post position* (also called the *pivot area*) at the free-throw line.

Note the numbers that accompany each position, since these are used in the play diagrams throughout the book—for example, 1 (or O1) is the point guard on offense, and X1 is the player defending 1. Again, note that position roles are meant to be fluid—adapting themselves to circumstances and player skills—not rigid and unvarying. Any coach welcomes a forward who can bury outside jump shots or a guard who can grab rebounds, while a guard who never drives to the basket or a forward who never attempts an outside shot makes his team's offense easier to predict and defend against.

To make it easy to understand the concepts, plays, offenses, and defenses presented in the book, we've included many diagrams. The diagrams use the symbols shown in the diagram key.

Offensive Formations

An *offensive formation* (or *offensive set*) tells the players where they should be at the start of a play. The plays in this book start from a few basic sets:

1-2-2 formation. This is also sometimes referred to as the 3-2 formation. This versatile formation consists of a point (1), two wings (2, 3), and two corners (4, 5). The two corners can also move toward their respective low post positions, leaving three players on the perimeter and two nearer the blocks, which is why some coaches call this the 3-2 Offensive Set or the 3-out, 2-in formation. Many of the plays in this book start with this formation. This is a practice-friendly formation because you can practice many plays— including give-and-go plays—using only part of the formation; for example, only two or three players instead of all five.

2-1-2 formation. This offensive set places the two guards (1, 2) between the wing position and the top of the circle, one on either side. A third player (usually the small forward, 3)

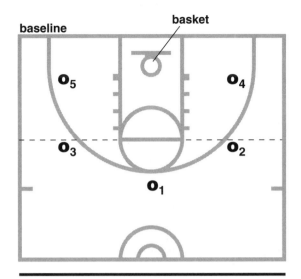

1-2-2 formation.

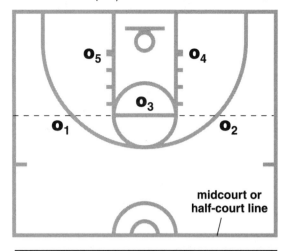

2-1-2 formation.

1-3-1 formation.

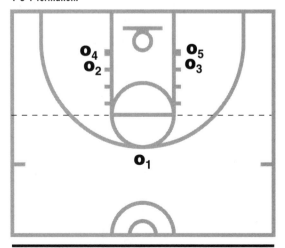

Stack set.

is near the foul line at the high post or pivot area, and the power forward and center (4, 5) are at the low post positions.

1-3-1 formation. This formation puts your point guard (1) at the point, your 2 guard and a forward (3) at the wings, the other forward (4) at the high post or pivot, and the center (5) at the low post.

Stack set. In this formation, your point guard (1) is at the point, with two players (one immediately in back of the other—2, 4) on or near one of the blocks. The other two players (3, 5) start in the same manner on or near the other block.

2-3 formation. This formation puts your two guards (1, 2) between the wing position and the top of the circle, one on either side. Your forwards (3, 4) begin at the corners, with the center (5) on one of the blocks. (See page 14.)

1-4 formation. In this formation the point guard (1) is at the point, and the other players position themselves along the baseline. Players 2 and 3 start at the corners, with the larger players 4 and 5 on the blocks. (See page 14.)

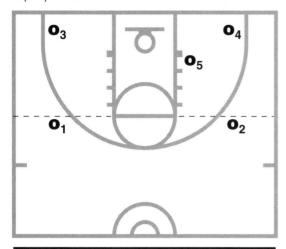

2-3 formation.

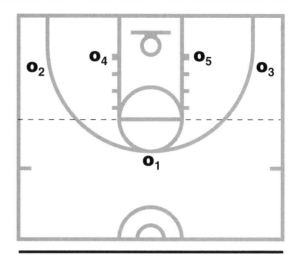

1-4 formation.

Principles of Offense

Perhaps the most fundamental division in a *half-court offense* (an offense executed once the team advances into the frontcourt) is the one between a continuity play and a set play. The continuity offense and zone offense plays presented later in this chapter are generically called continuity plays. A *continuity play* is simply a sequence of player and ball movements that repeats itself until a scoring opportunity opens up. This approach has distinct advantages, particularly for a youth team:

- It provides a framework and a pattern for your offense—a welcome relief from having young players cluster around the ball, dribble to no purpose with their backs to the basket, or give up their dribble deep in a corner and then give up the ball to a double-team.

- It involves all five players and prevents the defense from keying on your best players.

- It provides passing, dribbling, and scoring opportunities for every player, keeping their heads in the game, enhancing their growth in and through the game, and giving them pride of accomplishment—and isn't that what it's all about?

- It teaches fundamental principles such as spacing, purposeful movement, entry passes, and others.

- It teaches such fundamentals of offensive teamwork as the give-and-go and setting screens.

- Since there is usually no shot clock in youth play, you don't have to worry about a clock violation. The continuity sequence can repeat itself indefinitely until a scoring opportunity appears.

- Because it's a repeating pattern, it's easier for the kids to learn and you don't have to call instructions from the bench. Parents will marvel at the smooth-running efficiency of your team!

We recommend that you teach your players two to four continuity plays: one or two to use against a man-to-man defense, and one or two to use against a zone defense.

But what if your continuity offense stops working? What if it fails to create scoring opportunities? What if it becomes too predictable and the other team learns how to defend it and create turnovers from it? This shouldn't happen if your players continue to work on their skills and their initiative—ball fakes, step fakes, crisp passes, sharp cuts and drives, effective screens, and good open shots. Your athletes should make purposeful and aggressive movements, rather than go though the motions—the only exception is a slower movement to lull the defender before making an explosive move to the basket or the ball. But if despite best efforts, your continuity offense bogs down, you can try calling a set play from the bench.

Unlike a continuity play, a *set play* has an end. If it doesn't result in a scoring opportunity, the offense must reset before running another play. The advantages of a set play are:

- It can be designed to get the ball into the hands of your best player or players.
- It can be designed to attack unskilled defenders or a zone defense's areas of weakness.
- One or two well-executed set plays can create scoring opportunities over and over again, especially in a youth league, and can alter the tenor of a game.

Chapters 2 through 8 cover a wide range of set plays, including basic set plays, give-and-go plays, backdoor plays, pick-and-roll plays, scissor plays, baseline screen plays, and low post plays. Teach your players two or three of these—certainly no more than a handful. Choose plays that are well matched to what your most accomplished players do best.

In addition, you'll need a few plays for special situations: a fast-break opportunity, beating a backcourt press, and inbounding the ball from a sideline or baseline. You'll find these in Chapters 9 and 10. One of each should suffice, except that you might want to teach two to four plays for inbounding the ball from the offensive baseline—one or two to use against a man-to-man defense and one or two to use against a zone defense.

Resist the temptation to try to teach or make your players memorize every play or even most of the plays in this book. Rather, browse the book to select the handful of plays that your team can learn readily and execute well. Then build from there.

For example, all of the give-and-go plays presented in this book are derived from the same basic play. Chapter 3, the give-and-go chapter, shows you how the various permutations can be executed from different positions or angles on the court or used in different situations. The same can be said for the backdoor plays, the pick-and-roll plays, and so on. Therefore, you can first use this book to teach your players the basic version of the give-and-go and/or some of the other play categories. Once they master the basic version, you can (as the season progresses and as the need arises) use this book to show your players how they can vary the basic play to suit a situation.

Keep in mind the following principles when teaching the strategies in this book:

Spacing. A clogged-up area of the court not only limits scoring opportunities but leads to confusion and turnovers. It's quite common for the players on a youth team to converge on the ball, even if the ball handler is in good control. This draws all the defenders toward the ball as well, increasing the chances of a steal or other turnover. While you never want to discourage assertiveness or good hustle, you should teach your team that good spacing helps spread out the defense and makes it a bit harder for the defenders to help each other out. A 12- to 15-foot passing distance between offensive players is a good rule of thumb to follow. Spacing is an important component of all the offensive formations (offensive sets) and plays in this book.

Movement. This is the corollary to spacing. Plays are designed to use ball and player movement to create defensive lapses or gaps, and therefore scoring opportunities. The continuity offenses on pages 21–23 are good examples of simple and effective ways for youth teams to use continuous movement to create scoring opportunities for the entire team, not just the team's best player. Even the Get Open! Plays use player movements to free up players to receive the first pass to begin a play. You never want to have your best player, or any player, dribble the ball without purpose while other players stand around. Not only is that boring, it also makes the defense's job too easy. If your team can't get a play to work on the right-hand side of the court, reverse the ball and try to execute that play or another play from the left side of the court. Ball and player movement make your offense less predictable and harder to defend.

Patience. There is generally no shot clock in youth basketball. Even in professional basketball, which has a 24-second shot clock, it's bad basketball for the ball handler to dribble the ball into the frontcourt and then immediately heave up a long-distance shot. Remind your team to be patient and to utilize spacing, movement, and good shot selection. An open shot is better than taking a shot with a defender's hand in your face, and a shot from close range is almost always better than a shot from the perimeter. If a player is double-teamed, that means that a teammate may be open for a pass and an open shot. But remind your players to use common sense. For example, a tall player who has just made an offensive rebound might be better off immediately taking a close-range shot against a defender, and perhaps drawing a foul in the process, than kicking the ball out to a player on the perimeter.

And while basketball is a game that places a premium on explosive athletic ability—the quick cut to the basket, the quick release of a jump shot, etc.—patience even has a role in the execution of fundamental skills. If a play calls for a screen, the cutter has to wait for the screen to be set before he or she can use it to cut to the basket. Otherwise, the screen doesn't work. Yes, your athletes should play aggressively and fast, but rushed or panicked movements lead to bad decisions, bad shots, and turnovers.

Assertiveness. Patience is a virtue, but on the other hand, you don't want to stifle creativity or assertiveness. Remind your athletes that the plays are a means to an end, with the end being the creation of a scoring opportunity. Plays, which are mostly half-court offenses, are not meant to be robotically executed. If the team sees a fast-break opportunity, then it should try to take advantage of it. And if a scoring opportunity presents itself in mid-play— a gaping hole just begging for the ball handler to drive to the basket, for example—then he or she should exploit the opening and drive to the basket.

Get Open! Plays

It's important for youth players to understand that unless they get open to receive the ball, the intended play will never start. This is true whether the team runs a continuity offense or a set play. Therefore, here we'll introduce movements designed to help players get open so that the actual play can begin. Get Open! Plays are not "plays" in the traditional sense, but it's useful to think of and teach them as such, because mastery of these movements will provide the lubrication that sets the machine (your young team) in motion and creates scoring opportunities.

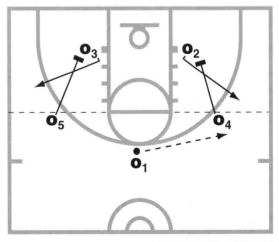

Point Pass to Wing Using a Down Screen (1-2-2 Set)

Run the Play

Players 4 and 5 down screen for 2 and 3. A *down screen* is a play in which a player comes down from the perimeter to screen for a player in the low post area.

Players 2 and 3 use the screen and break to the wing.

Player 1 makes the entry pass to either 2 or 3 to begin the play (such as the Give-and-Go, Screen Away, etc.).

Point pass to wing.

Scoring opportunities. If 2 or 3 receives the ball on the wing, he or she looks to shoot the open medium-range jumper. Remember that being open means being far enough from the defender to *square up* (to pivot so the shoulders and feet face the basket) and take an unobstructed shot. If a young player receives the ball near the 3-point arc, he is probably too far from the basket to shoot with proper mechanics even if no one is guarding him.

If 2 or 3 receives the ball on the wing, chances are he'll have a good passing angle to 4 or 5 set up in the low post. If 2 or 3 is able to get the ball into the low post, then 4 or 5 looks to make a low post move and score a layup or power move basket.

Focus on Fundamentals

Players 2 and 3 should wait for and then use the screen before breaking to the wing.

Spacing. Players shouldn't stand around. The only way to get open is to keep moving. If denied the ball after using the screen to pop out to the wing, 2 or 3 should down screen for 4 or 5, who in turn breaks to the wing.

Some young players have a tendency to down screen an area rather than the defender. Down screens work only if you're able to block the defender's path. First find the defender, and then down screen him.

Defend the Play

The defenders should communicate who will cover the *screen cutter* (the player who uses a screen set for him by cutting shoulder to shoulder with the screener) and who will cover the *screener* (the player who sets a screen).

If the ball is at the top of the key, all the defensive players except X1 (the point guard's defender) will be playing close man-to-man defense, attempting to *deny the ball* (prevent the offensive player from receiving a pass). In theory, nobody will be playing *weak-side help defense* (defensive players on the side of the court the ball is not on, helping out by playing closer to the side of the court the ball is on) because the ball is on or near the imaginary line running from one basket to the other that splits the court into its left and right halves. This means that the lane is more or less open to penetration by the point guard. Therefore it's important for X1 to play tough on-ball defense, and pressure the point guard to go to his "weaker" side (ball handlers usually have a preference for driving to the left or the right depending on which side he is more comfortable with; it's usually his left side if right-handed, and vice versa).

If all the other defenders are denying the ball, this means that a player guarding a screener (initially, 4 or 5) will be more or less in front of the screener. If a switch is called, he may find it difficult to switch to defend against a screen cutter who decides not to use the screen to cut to the wing and instead pops outside to receive a pass from the point guard for a jump shot. If this happens, instead of switching defenders, it may be better for the defender to follow the screen cutter through the down screen by taking a series of short steps to *fight over the screen* (to stick out his hips and torso and then step over the wide-leg stance of the screener).

Of course, you may wish to adapt your defensive strategy to the skills of your opponent. If your opponent has a great penetration dribbler at the 1 position, great outside shooters, or great low post players, you'll want to adjust accordingly. Keep in mind, however, that any defensive adjustment you make is likely to have pitfalls that may offset any benefits gained. For example, coaches sometimes like to have their wing defenders *sag off* the offensive wing players a bit to help X1 defend against the penetration drive to the basket. The problem with this strategy is that wing players are often the best outside shooters on the team. Sagging in this way leaves the offensive wing players open to receive a pass and make an open jump shot. On the other hand, over-playing your wing players may leave the defense vulnerable to backdoor cuts to the basket. A *backdoor cut* is an offensive play in which a player on the perimeter steps away from the basket, drawing the defender with him, and suddenly cuts to the basket behind the defender for a pass.

Allowing an easy entry pass to be made to the wing causes other problems as well. Many hard-to-defend plays are initiated by a wing player with the ball—for example, the *pick-and-roll*, a two-person play in which one offensive player sets a screen *(pick)* on the ball handler's defender and cuts *(rolls)* to the basket after the ball handler drives by the screen. Or the wing player can simply dump the ball down low for a forward or center to make a low post power move basket, and perhaps get fouled to boot! Sometimes, at least at the youth basketball level, it's best not to overthink these issues. Allow your players to learn the fundamentals of good straight-up man-to-man defense. If you make defensive adjustments, make sure that the adjustments, which are meant to be temporary, do not turn into permanent bad habits.

Point Pass to Wing Using a Back Screen (1-2-2 Set)

Run the Play

Players 4 and 5 back screen for players 2 and 3. A *back screen* is an offensive play in which a player comes from the low post to set a screen for a player on the perimeter.

Players 2 and 3 use the screen and cut to the basket.

Players 4 and 5 *pop out* (move to the pivot, high post, or wing areas) to receive the ball.

Player 1 makes the entry pass to either 4 or 5 to begin the play (such as the Give-and-Go, Screen Away, etc.).

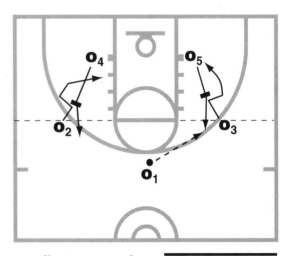

Point pass to wing using a back screen.

Scoring opportunities. Back screens are often an effective way to free up screeners (4 and 5, in this instance), but 1 should also look to pass to 2 or 3 if either one is cutting to the basket for a layup.

Focus on Fundamentals

Spacing. Timing is important. Players 2 and 3 have to wait for 4 and 5 to set their back screens before cutting to the basket. Players 4 and 5 pop out after 2 and 3 use their screens. If the play doesn't yield an entry pass, the players can repeat it or run one of the other Get Open! Plays.

Player 1 may need to take a quick dribble or two to improve his passing angle.

Defend the Play

Back screens are not as common as down screens in youth league play, but remind your players that the key to defending *any* screen is communication. The defenders need to communicate who will cover the screen cutter and who will cover the screener. The defenders should not automatically assume that 4 or 5 will pop out to receive the pass. If 2 and 3 clear the lane to create space after cutting to the basket, then 4 or 5 could also cut to the basket.

Down Screen with High Post Entry Pass (1-2-2 Set)

Run the Play

Players 4 and 5 down screen for 2 and 3.

Players 2 and 3 use the screen and break to the wing.

Players 4 and 5 pop out to the high post.

Player 1 makes the entry pass to 4 or 5 to begin the play (such as two or three backdoor cuts to the basket).

Scoring opportunities. In youth league play, screeners often stick around after the screen cutter has used the screen. This may result in missed opportunities or clogged-up lanes. But in this case, 4 and 5 pop out to the high post area. All of this movement may cause the defenders to get confused and result in unnecessary double coverage of either the screener or screen cutter. Player 4 (or 5) or 2 (or 3) may find herself wide open for a short jump shot.

Down screen with high post entry pass.

Focus on Fundamentals

Spacing. Most youth teams expect and therefore overplay the entry pass to the wing. If an entry pass to the wing is not available, then 1 can pass the ball to 4 or 5, who has popped out to the high post.

As soon as 4 or 5 receives the ball in the high post, 2 or 3 can make a backdoor cut to the basket.

Defend the Play

The defenders should communicate who will cover the screen cutter and who will cover the screener.

Continuity Offenses

Some youth basketball teams have good success understanding and executing *continuity offenses*, which rely on continuous movement and keep repeating until a good scoring opportunity is created. Remember that a set play runs once, and if it (or the second option) doesn't work the first time, the offense has to reset itself before attempting something else.

Since youth leagues usually don't have shot clocks, as long as your team is patient and relentless in its player and ball movements, you have a good chance to find and exploit a lapse in defense for a scoring opportunity.

We'll discuss two simple continuity offenses here, the Give-and-Go Continuity Offense and the Screen-Away Continuity Offense. Note that the give-and-go and the screen away can also be run as set plays, and are discussed as such in Chapters 2 and 3.

Give-and-Go Continuity Offense (1-2-2 Set)

Run the Play

Player 2 *V-cuts* to receive an entry pass — takes his defender toward the basket, then plants his inside foot, pivots, and cuts sharply back toward the perimeter, but this time closer to 1 than he was before the V-cut.

Player 1 makes the entry pass to 2. Player 1 takes a step to the weak side with his weak-side foot, then cuts to the basket.

Scoring opportunities. Player 2 can pass to 1 for a layup, or pass to 5 for a low post move to the basket, or drive to the basket if there is an opening.

If none of these is open, 2 can pass to 3, who has meanwhile moved to the point to fill the spot vacated by 1. At the same

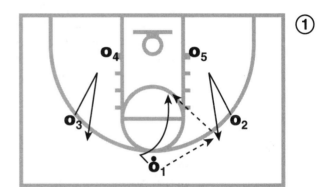

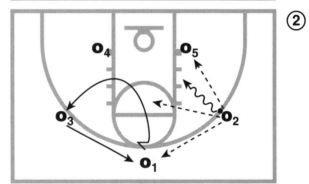

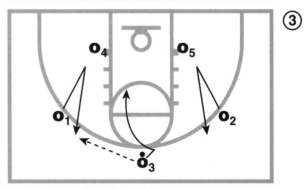

Give-and-go continuity offense. ① Player 2 V-cuts to receive the pass from 1. ② Player 2 can pass to 1 or 5, or try for a layup. ③ If 3 gets the ball, he can pass to either wing.

time, 1 cuts to the opposite wing to fill the open spot vacated by 3. Repeat the sequence with 3 as point, passing to either wing.

Or if 2's defender sags off 2 in anticipation of the cut by 1, 2 may find himself open for a short jump shot.

Focus on Fundamentals

Spacing. Player 2 needs to push off with his right foot to V-cut to his left. As 1 cuts to the basket, he should use his lead hand to give 2 a passing target. Player 2 may need to take a quick dribble or two to improve his passing angle to 1. Player 2 should not pick up his dribble until he is certain that he can make the pass to the cutter.

Player 2 should be aware of the defense providing weak-side help. Player 2 should never pass into traffic. If the lane is clogged with help, then he should pass the ball to another player who has rotated to the top of the key to start another play.

After 1 cuts to the basket but does not receive the pass, he should clear the lane to maintain proper player spacing on the court.

Defend the Play

Player X1 should use good on-ball defense against 1. If 1 is in his *triple threat position* (the bent-knees stance that allows the player three options: dribble, pass, or shoot), the defender should take care to prevent 1 from driving to his strong side.

Player X2 should deny 2 the ball by keeping one hand and one foot on the *passing line* (the straight line between the passer and the receiver), while simultaneously keeping an eye on the ball and 2. He also should stay alert for a backdoor pass from 1 to 2 cutting to the basket.

Pass and Screen-Away Continuity Offense (1-2-2 Set)

Run the Play

Player 1 makes the entry pass to 2.

Player 5 sets a cross screen for 4 at the opposite low post. A *cross screen* is a movement in which a player cuts across the lane to screen for a teammate. Player 4 uses the screen to cut across the lane.

Meanwhile 1 *screens away* (screens to the side opposite his entry pass) for 3. Player 3 uses the screen to cut to the basket or into the lane.

Scoring opportunities. If 4 receives the ball, he should be ready to make a power move to the basket, especially if a previous screen creates a mismatch and a smaller defender is covering him in the low post.

Neither 4 nor 5 should hang around in the paint long enough to create a 3-second violation.

Player 2 can pass to 3 for a layup or jump shot, or to 4 for a low post move to the basket. If neither of these is open, 2 can pass to 3, who has moved to the point to fill the spot vacated by 1.

Repeat the sequence with 3 as point, passing to either wing.

Focus on Fundamentals

Spacing. If any cutter is denied, he should immediately cross screen or down screen to maintain the 1-2-2 set. All cutters should wait for the screen and then use the screen to get open.

Defend the Play

The defenders should communicate who will cover the screen cutter and who will cover the screener.

Players X4 and X5 should be ready to defend a low post move to the basket since cross screens are often used to create low post opportunities.

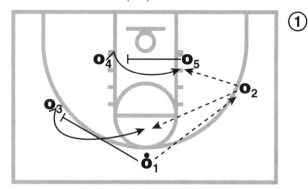

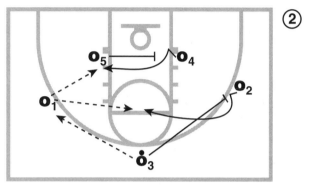

Zone Offense

We believe that it's critical for young players to learn how to play *man-to-man defense*, in which each defender guards a specific player or *man*. Therefore, we do not encourage teaching youth teams how to play *zone defense*, in which defenders are assigned areas, or *zones*, of the court rather than being assigned players to guard. That said, you can't control what kind of defense your opponent will use against your team, so in this section we introduce some basic concepts of *zone offense*.

Zone Defenses Your Team Might Encounter

A defender in a zone defense is assigned an area rather than a player to guard, and she must guard any opposing player who enters that zone, with or without the ball. As with offensive sets, zone defenses are designated by the positions of the players in their zones. The best zone defenders are able to move quickly within their zones in response to player and ball movements. The best zone offenses, on the other hand, are able to take advantage of inherent gaps or structural weaknesses in a zone defense using dribble penetration and other techniques discussed below.

One-guard fronts are zone defenses that have one defender at or near the top of the circle. These include the 1-2-2 and 1-3-1 zone defenses.

Pass and screen-away continuity offense. ① Player 1 passes to 2 and 5 sets a cross screen for 4. ② Player 3 is point.

The result of dribble penetration is an open teammate.
(Bruce Curtis)

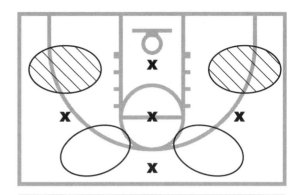

The defenders in a 1-3-1 zone defense initially position themselves much like the offensive players in a 1-3-1 offensive set. Only one defender has the main responsibility to cover the baseline, so the two crosshatched areas along the baseline are the obvious areas of weakness.

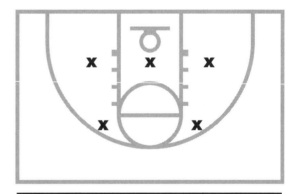

The defenders in a 2-3 zone defense initially position themselves much like the offensive players in a 2-3 offensive set. Since there are only two defenders near the top, the top middle and wings are areas of weakness in the 2-3 zone.

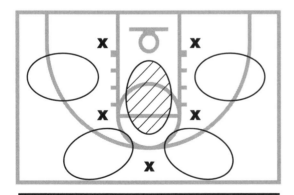

The defenders in a 1-2-2 zone defense initially position themselves much like the offensive players in a 1-2-2 offensive set. The oval areas indicate structural weaknesses in the defense, particularly the middle area indicated by the vertical crosshatched oval.

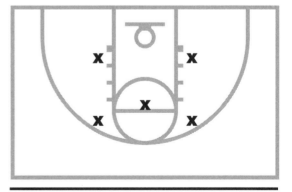

The defenders in a 2-1-2 zone defense initially position themselves much like the offensive players in a 2-1-2 offensive set.

Two-guard fronts are zone defenses that have two players (usually guards) at the top. These include 2-3 and 2-1-2 zone defenses.

Attacking a One-Guard Zone Defense

Run the Play

Player 1 dribbles into the seam. (The typical reaction is that X1 and X2 will converge on 1.) Player 3 cuts behind her defender into the lane, 5 posts up, and 2 and 4 are in position to receive a pass.

Player 1 can pass to any of the players, but 4 is the best option since 4 is in the best position to attack the main area of weakness in a 1-2-2 zone defense. (If the defenders employ a 1-3-1 zone defense, then the offensive players in the short corners along the baseline are in the best position to exploit the zone's weaknesses.)

Depending on how the defense reacts, 4 can pass to 3 or 5 down low, to 2 on the opposite wing, or even shoot the ball or drive toward the basket.

Scoring opportunities. If 4 passes to 3 or 5 down low, 3 or 5 can make a low post move to score a basket.

Alternatively, after passing to 3 or 5, 4 can cut to the basket or set a screen for either low post player. If 4 sets the screen for the low post player with the ball, the ball handler can use the screen to free herself for a power move layup. If 4 sets the screen for the player without the ball, that player can use the screen to cut into the lane to receive a pass from the opposite corner.

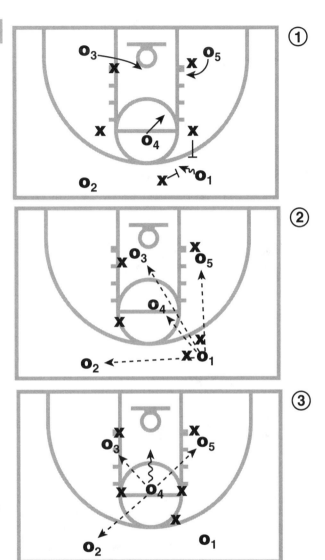

Attacking a one-guard zone defense. ① Player 1 is under pressure as play begins. ② Player 1 can pass to any teammate, but 4 is the best choice. ③ Player 4 can pass to 3, 5, or 2, or try to score.

Focus on Fundamentals

Position your players with two guards up top, a good passing forward (4) in the high post or pivot area, and the other players at the corners. This is similar to the 2-1-2 offensive set and places 1, 2, and 4 in good positions to attack the main areas of weakness.

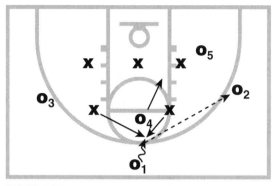

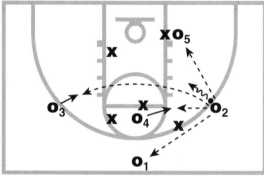

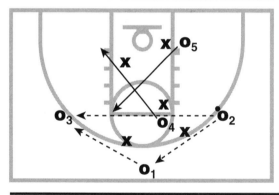

Attacking a two-guard zone defense. ① Player 1 can pass to 2 or 4.
② If 2 gets the ball, he has several options. ③ Player 2 passes back to 1.

Attacking a Two-Guard Zone Defense

Run the Play

Player 1 dribbles into the seam. (The typical reaction is that X1 and X2 will converge on 1.) Player 1 can pass to an open wing player or to 4 in the high post.

If 1 passes to 2, then 5 posts up on the block and 4 tries to get open on the elbow area closest to the ball. Player 1 then goes back to the top of the key area, and gets ready for the ball to be return passed to him.

Scoring opportunities. Depending on how the defense reacts, 2 can pass to 5, and 5 can make a low post move to score a basket.

Alternatively, 2 can pass the ball to 4, drive to the basket, or shoot the open jump shot, if available.

Otherwise, 2 passes the ball back to 1, and the others reposition themselves to execute the play on the other side of the court. In this case, 4 and 5 make diagonal cuts to switch positions—4 will end up near the block area, and 5 takes the high post area near the foul line.

Focus on Fundamentals

In youth basketball, use a one-guard offense to play against a two-guard zone defense. Position your players with one guard up top, a good passing forward (4) in the high post or pivot area, 2 and 3 on the wings, and 5 near one of the low blocks. This is similar to the 1-3-1 offensive set. Players 2 and 3 should position themselves more or less on a line between the wing defenders and the baseline, so that they are in a better position to attack the seam between the wing defenders and the baseline defenders.

There are certain offensive principles you can employ against a zone defense.

Attack the areas of weakness. As discussed above, all zone defenses have inherent areas of weakness, typically in the "gray areas" between two zones. Use this baseball analogy to help your players think of how to attack these areas of weakness. If a baseball is hit squarely to the center fielder, the fielders are in no doubt as to who should field the ball. If a baseball is hit into right field, there is again no question as to whose responsibility the ball is. But what about a baseball hit into the gap between center field and right field? Experienced outfielders will know which player should field the ball based on such factors as who's on base, which fielder has the better range and the better throwing arm, and whether the center fielder or right fielder is left-handed or right-handed. But at the youth level, balls hit into the gap often cause confusion for the outfielders. Because nobody calls for the ball, it often falls to the ground for a base hit. If your basketball team wants to be successful against a zone defense, the perimeter players should think of themselves as baseballs. Attack the seams between the zones with the dribble (called *dribble penetration*). In the best-case scenario, a confused defense will not converge, and the ball handler will find a clear lane to the basket. And if two defenders converge to cover the ball handler, somebody else must be open.

Movement. Ball movement is critical to success against a zone defense. As in the continuity offense, keep moving the ball until a good scoring opportunity arises. Use dribble penetrations and ball fakes to open up the defense. Right-handed players tend to favor their right side, and left-handed players their left side, since going the other way requires them to dribble with their off hands, but remind your players to mix it up—reverse the ball and use both sides of the zone offense. Weak-side players can *flash* (cut) into open areas of the zone to receive a pass. Also, keep in mind that zone defenders are almost always mentally in help mode; they often face the ball and sometimes lose track of where opponents are. For example, 3 may be able to exploit this and cut behind the defender into an open area for a possible pass.

Fast-break opportunities. Sometimes the best strategy against a zone defense is to fast-break the ball to the frontcourt before the defense has time to set up their zones. See Chapter 9 for more on fast breaks.

CHAPTER 2

Basic Set Plays

Chapter 1 introduced several continuity plays. These will give structure, pattern, and purposeful movement to your offense, transforming your players from a temporary playground agglomeration into a real team. Continuity plays also teach such fundamental precepts as spacing, screening, the entry pass, the give-and-go, and flexible attack while providing a framework for improving passing, dribbling, moving without the ball, and shooting. Continuity plays involve all five players and provide a great foundation for an offense.

But there may come times against a zone defense or against fast, aggressive, well-coached defenders when your continuity offense bogs down and starts producing as many turnovers as scoring opportunities. When this happens, you need a handful of set plays to get the ball into the hands of your best players, to attack the other team's zone defense or its weaker defenders, or simply to change the tempo and scramble the predictability of your offense.

This chapter contains the simplest set plays. They are easy to understand and can be practiced in the context of small-sided 2-on-2 or 3-on-3 games. We recommend that you teach these to your players.

Back cut to layup.

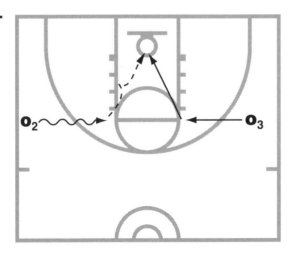

Back Cut to Layup (1-2-2 Set)

Run the Play

Starting from opposite sides of the court near the foul line extended, 2 dribbles toward 3.

At the same time, 3 takes a few steps toward 2. If 3 is closely guarded, this may leave her defender in a trailing position and create an open lane toward the basket.

Player 3 then makes her *back cut*—she plants her outside foot and cuts sharply to the basket.

Scoring opportunity. Player 2 passes the ball to 3 for a layup.

Focus on Fundamentals

This play works better if X3 is closely guarding 3. It works less well if X3 is guarding 3 loosely and cheating toward the ball side of the court—playing weak-side help defense.

Player 2 will be passing the ball into the lane, and a bounce pass often works best in this situation.

While looking to execute this play, 2 should also remain aware of other opportunities that may arise to drive to the basket or to pass the ball to another open teammate.

As always, your players should understand that merely going through the play's motions isn't automatically going to generate a scoring opportunity. Sudden speed changes, sharp cuts, crisp passes, fakes, strong dribbles, and a readiness to adapt to what the defense is offering are what get the job done.

Defend the Play

Player X3 should be wary of overplaying 3 when the ball is on the other side of the court. If X3 guards her man too closely, she won't have enough time to recover if and when 3 cuts to the basket. Player X3 also won't be in a good position to help out if 2 decides to drive to the basket.

Screen Dribble to Handoff (1-2-2 Set)

Run the Play

Player 1 dribbles toward 2, and 2 moves toward 1.

As 1's outside shoulder draws even with 2's inside shoulder, 1 hands off the ball to 2 while setting a screen for 2.

Scoring opportunity. Player 2 uses the screen to drive to the basket or take a jump shot.

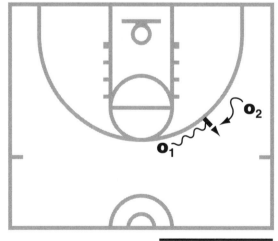

Screen dribble to handoff.

Focus on Fundamentals

Sometimes an intervening defender will prevent player 1 from passing close to 2 and handing 2 the ball. In this case, 1 should avoid forcing the handoff or making a sudden short toss. Rather, 1 should pick up his dribble and set a screen for 2, then wait for 2 to use the screen and execute the Runaround (see the next play).

As 2 takes the handoff, he should be ready to exploit any immediate opening to drive to the basket or take an unguarded jump shot. If no such opening exists, he should grab the ball and get into a triple threat position.

If 2 does not have an opening, 1 has the option (after setting the screen) to roll to the basket for a pass from 2.

Defend the Play
Players X1 and X2 need to communicate who will cover the screen cutter and who will cover the screener.

Player X2 should try to deny 2 the ball, but should also be wary of 2 cutting backdoor to the basket.

Second Options
If after taking the handoff, 2 does not have an opening to drive to the basket or take a jump shot, 2 can pass the ball inside to 1, who has rolled to the basket after setting his pick (screen).

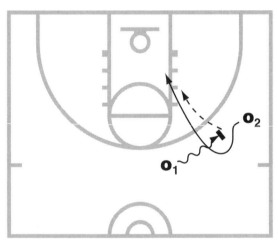

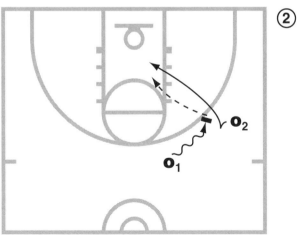

① Runaround. ② Runaround alternative.

Runaround (1-2-2 Set)

Run the Play
Player 1 dribbles toward 2 while 2 moves toward 1 as if to execute the Screen Dribble to Handoff (see previous play).

If a defender between 1 and 2 prevents the handoff from taking place, 1 picks up his dribble and sets a screen for 2.

Player 2 runs around the screen to cut to the basket.

Player 1 passes the ball to 2 for the layup.

Focus on Fundamentals
While making his cut, 2 should hold his hands up to give 1 a target to pass to.

Player 1 makes either an overhead or bounce pass to 2.

Diagram 1 shows 2 running around the screen. Diagram 2 shows that 2 could fake the runaround to draw X2 into the screen, and then cut to the basket in front of the screen. By the way, "running around" merely refers to the direction the screen cutter moves; he should still use the screen by running hard shoulder to shoulder with the screener.

The weak-side offensive players should remain in motion to occupy the weak-side defenders and prevent them from obstructing the ball-side play. By moving, they might also be able to create an impromptu opportunity to cut to the basket and receive a pass from 1.

As always, 1, like any player with the ball, should remain alert for any scoring opportunity involving any player. It is a mistake to concentrate on the play at hand to the exclusion of other scoring opportunities.

Defend the Play

Players X1 and X2 need to communicate who will cover the screen cutter and who will cover the screener.

Handoff and Shoot over Screen (1-3-1 Set)

Run the Play

Player 2 V-cuts to the wing to receive the pass from 1.

Player 1 takes a step toward the basket but then moves toward 2, dropping behind 2 for a handoff or short pass.

Player 2 hands or passes the ball to 1 and then sets a screen for 1.

Scoring opportunity. Player 1 looks to take a shot over the screen set by 2.

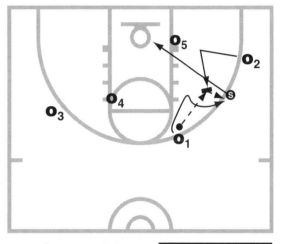

Handoff and shoot over screen.

Focus on Fundamentals

Players commonly use V-cuts to get open to receive a pass. A player executes a V-cut by taking a short step or series of steps in one direction (more or less toward the basket) and then pushing off the inside foot (the foot toward the basket) to shift his momentum away from the basket to receive the ball. The player has to bend his knees a bit to gather momentum for the explosive push off his inside foot. In the diagram, 2 would push off with his right foot to V-cut to his left. To make a V-cut to cut to his right, 2 would push off with his left foot to cut to the right.

When 1 moves toward 2, he should make it appear that he is going to set a screen for 2. When X1 gets caught in the screen, 1 cuts behind 2, ready to receive a handoff or short underhand shovel pass from 2.

It's best if 1 can shoot the ball over the screen set by 2 without first having to dribble. Young players may find it difficult to square up to the basket on the run, however, so they may need to take a quick dribble before shooting the jump shot.

Player 1 has many options besides shooting the ball after receiving the handoff or short pass from 2. He can use a variety of fake-out moves (see pages 100–105) together with the screen set by 2 in order to create opportunities to drive to the basket.

Defend the Play

Players X1 and X2 need to communicate who will cover the screen cutter and who will cover the screener.

While a handoff often leads directly to a jump shot over 2's screen, the defenders should not overplay the jump shot. If a defender leaves the ground before the shooter does, it will be difficult for the defender to recover. It's better to give up an insufficiently contested jump shot than an uncontested drive to the basket.

Second Options

Scoring opportunity. If 1 is unable to take a shot or drive to the basket using the screen set by 2, 2 can roll to the basket. Player 1 can then pass the ball to 2 for a layup. Player 5 will need to clear the lane, and 3 will need to rotate to the top of the key.

Pass and screen away.

Pass and Screen Away (1-2-2 Set)

Run the Play

Player 1 makes the entry pass to 2, then screens away for 3.

Player 3 uses the screen and cuts to the basket.

Scoring opportunity. Player 2 passes the ball to 3 for a layup.

Focus on Fundamentals

A *screen away* occurs when a player passes the ball to a teammate on one side of the court, and then sets a screen away from the ball for a teammate on the other side of the floor.

When setting the screen, 1 jumps into position with both feet so that he isn't moving. Remember to remind your screener that he is not screening the general area that X3 is defending—in other words, 1 must find X3 and screen him. It's a good idea to have a coach or player act as X3 so that 1 can learn to set proper screens.

The diagram shows 3 cutting in front of/around the screen. If X3 anticipates the screen and commits to cutting through the screen, 3 may be in a good position to cut behind the screen, instead of in front of/around it.

Spacing. The cutter, 3 (and perhaps 1 as the second cutter—see the Second Options section below), needs to decide which corner he will rotate to after making his cut. This will depend on where 4 and 5 are at the time; 4 or 5 may have cut to the basket for a pass from 2.

Defend the Play

Players X1 and X3 need to communicate who will cover the screen cutter and who will cover the screener.

Player 1 always has the option to cut with a give-and-go (see Chapter 3) after making the entry pass to 2. Player X1 should be ready for this.

Second Options

After 3 uses the screen (set by 1) to cut into the lane and to the basket, 1 can spin into the lane as the second cutter. In the diagram, 1 has screened away to the right side of the court. Therefore, 1 spins by pivoting on the foot closest to the basket (his left foot) and taking a drop step with the other foot (his right foot) clockwise and toward the lane/basket. Player 2 looks to pass the ball to 1 if the first cutter (3) is not open.

Depending on the defender's position, 1 might be able to cut straight to the basket by pivoting on the foot closest to the basket (his left foot) and taking a step forward with the other foot (his right foot) counterclockwise toward the basket.

Scoring opportunities. Player 1 should be aware of X1's reaction as 1 makes his initial cut to the ball before cutting to the weak side to screen away. If X1 anticipates the screen away by moving toward 3, then 1 may be able run a give-and-go and cut straight to the basket. In this case, 2 can pass the ball to 1 for the layup.

Players 4 and 5 should be moving even though they are not the first or second options in this play. If 4 or 5 is able to fake and then beat X4 or X5 to the basket, then 2 can pass the ball to 4 or 5 for a layup. Additionally, by moving they may distract X4 or X5 and prevent them from helping defend against 3 or 1 cutting.

Pass and Down Screen Away (1-2-2 Set)

Run the Play

Player 1 makes the entry pass to 2, and then down screens for 5.

Player 4 clears the lane to create space for the play.

Player 5 uses the screen and cuts across the lane, ready to receive a pass into the low post.

Player 2 passes the ball to 5 for a power move/layup to the basket.

Focus on Fundamentals

Spacing. Player 4 clears the lane to the corner to create space for the play. Player 3 should rotate to the top of the key. If the play can't be made, then 2 can pass the ball to 3 and the team can reset for another play.

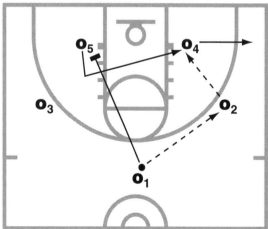

Pass and down screen away.

This play has to be executed quickly. Player 5 needs to clear the lane if he can't receive the ball and make the basket without incurring a 3-second violation. When 5 clears the lane, he can set up for a low post move on the right-side block, just outside the lane to avoid incurring a 3-second violation. Keep in mind that X4 will be in the vicinity, which may preclude this option.

Defend the Play

Players X1 and X5 need to communicate who will cover the screen cutter and who will cover the screener. Player 1 is usually the point guard, and 5 is usually the center, so X1 and X5 should be aware of a possible size mismatch if they switch coverage.

Player 1 has the option to pivot and receive the ball as the second cutter, provided he still has time before incurring a 3-second violation, and provided that he is not on the short end of a size mismatch in the low post. Keep in mind that post play is not just for your tallest players.

Give-and-Go Plays

Give-and-go plays are actually more accurately called give, go, and receive plays. Basically, a *give-and-go* is any play that involves a player passing the ball to a teammate (the *give*) and promptly cutting to the basket (the *go*). If she is able to shake off her defender, then she will be open to receive a return pass from her teammate and shoot a layup. It's a simple play that fits nicely with the concept that players without the ball on offense should always be moving—not standing around!

We introduced give-and-go plays in Chapter 1 as part of basic continuity offense. Give-and-go plays can be called as set plays, too, and can be executed in a variety of situations from different starting positions and angles on the floor, and can be practiced in small-sided formats. In addition, players should also look for on-the-fly give-and-go opportunities. In fact, anytime a player passes the ball to a teammate is a potential give-and-go situation. For example, let's say you instruct your point guard to start a Pass and Screen Away (see pages 32–33). No doubt he'll dutifully makes the entry pass to the wing. Lots of point guards will then automatically (but as instructed) cut in the opposite direction to screen away the weak-side wing player. But the point guard (and any player with the ball) should always consider the possibility of running a give-and-go. Encourage your playmakers (including *any* player with the ball, not just the point guard) to play spontaneously, and to make decisions without fear. In this case, if the point guard sees an opportunity to cut straight to the basket, or fake and then cut to the basket, he should do it. If he raises his hand and gives the wing player a good target, chances are the wing player will also see this scoring opportunity.

Basic Give-and-Go

Run the Play
Player 2 V-cuts to receive an entry pass from 1.

Player 1 takes a step to the weak side with his weak-side foot, and then cuts to the basket.

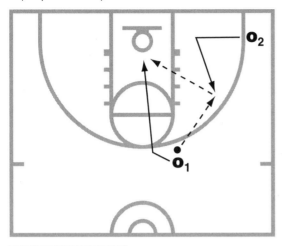

Basic give-and-go.

Scoring opportunity. Player 2 passes the ball to 1 for the layup.

Focus on Fundamentals
Player 2 should push off with his right foot to V-cut to his left. He may need to take a quick dribble or two to improve his passing angle to 1, and should not pick up his dribble until he is certain that he can make the pass to the cutter.

Player 2 also should be aware of the defense providing weak-side help and should never pass into traffic. If the lane is clogged with help, then 2 can pass the ball to another player who has rotated to the top of the key to start another play.

As 1 cuts to the basket, he should use his lead hand to give 2 a passing target. If he cuts to the basket but does not receive the pass, he should clear the lane to maintain proper player spacing on the court.

Defend the Play
Player X1 should use good on-ball defense against 1. If 1 is in his triple threat position, X1 should try to keep 1 from driving to his strong side.

Player X2 should deny 2 the ball by keeping one hand and one foot on the passing line while simultaneously keeping an eye on the ball and 2. He also should stay alert for a backdoor pass from 1 to 2 cutting to the basket.

Second Options
Scoring opportunity. If X2 sags off 2 in anticipation of the cut by 1, 2 may find himself open for a short jump shot.

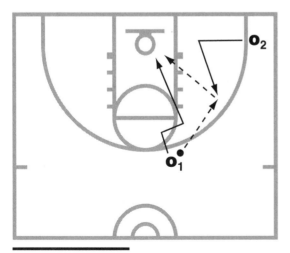

Basic give-and-go, ball side.

Basic Give-and-Go, Ball Side
Run the Play
Player 2 V-cuts to receive an entry pass from 1.

Player 1 takes a step to the weak side with his weak-side foot, cuts to receive the ball from 2, and then cuts to the basket.

Scoring opportunity. Player 2 passes the ball to 1 for the layup.

Focus on Fundamentals
By first taking a step to the weak side, and then cutting to the ball, 1 may be able to cut to the basket with X1 behind him instead of in front of him. This may make the return pass from 2 easier to make.

Give-and-Go with Back Screen

Run the Play

Player 1 makes the entry pass to 2.

Player 4 back screens for 1, who uses the screen to cut to the basket.

Scoring opportunity. Player 2 passes the ball to 1 for the layup.

Focus on Fundamentals

The pass from 1 to 2 to start the play is dangerous because it is across the court. If a defender is able to pick off the pass, she will have an uncontested layup at the other end of the court. Therefore, if needed, 1 should take a quick dribble or two to improve her passing angle to 2. Player 2 may need to make a V-cut to shake off X2 to receive the pass.

If X1 sags off 1 to help cover 2, 1 can cut directly to the basket without waiting for the screen.

Otherwise, 1 waits for the screen, and then cuts shoulder to shoulder around either side of the screen. Diagram 2 shows 1 cutting to the right of the screen. Player 1 can start her cut to the right; if X1 tries to follow 1 to the right through the screen and if X4 stays with 4, then 1 can switch directions and cut to the left side of the screen.

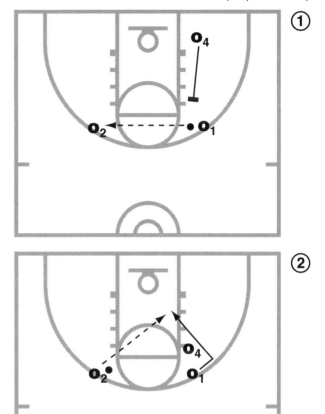

Give-and-go with back screen. ① Player 1 passes to 2. ② Player 1 uses the back screen to cut to the basket.

Defend the Play

Player X1 should play good on-ball defense against 1. If 1 is in her triple threat position, then X1 should try to keep 1 from driving to her strong side.

Player X2's priority is denying the ball and helping out as needed, not trying to intercept the ball for a layup at the other basket. Otherwise, 1 could fake a pass to 2, prompting an overanxious and gullible X2 to try to intercept the pass. As soon as X2 commits, 2 can cut in the other direction to the basket.

After 1 passes the ball to 2 on the opposite side of the court, X1 may need to play weak-side help defense, and position herself more or less between 1 and 2, keeping in mind that 1 might cut straight to the basket.

Players X1 and X4 need to communicate who will cover the screen cutter and who will cover the screener.

Second Options

Scoring opportunities. After 1 cuts into the lane but does not receive the pass, 1 goes to the left corner. If 1 is open, 2 can passes the ball to 1 for a short jump shot.

After setting the screen, 4 may find herself open because X1 and X4 are both covering 1 as she cuts into the lane. If 4 is open, 2 can pass the ball to 4 for a short jump shot. Player 4 can also roll to the basket as the second cutter after setting the screen.

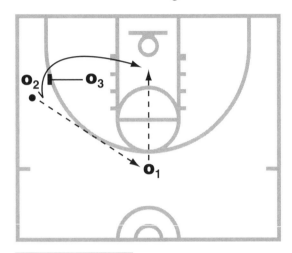

Give-and-go with baseline screen.

Give-and-Go with Baseline Screen

Run the Play

Player 2 passes the ball to 1.

Player 3 *baseline screens* for 2—he sets a screen near the blocks along the baseline.

Player 2 uses the screen and cuts to the basket.

Scoring opportunity. Player 1 passes the ball to 2 for the layup.

Focus on Fundamentals

Player 3 should leave enough room to allow 2 to cut around the baseline side of the screen. If 3 sets the screen too close to the baseline, the defense will be able to anticipate that 2 will have no choice but to cut in front of the screen.

Player 1 may need to make a quick dribble or two to improve his passing angle. Player 1 should not pick up his dribble until he is certain he can make the pass to the cutter.

Defend the Play

Players X2 and X3 need to communicate who will cover the screen cutter and who will cover the screener.

Second Options

Scoring opportunities. If X3 is behind 3, then 1 may be able to pass the ball directly to 3 for a low post move to the basket. Therefore, it's important for 2 to wait until 3 sets the screen before making his cut.

The diagram shows 2 cutting to the baseline side of the screen. If X2 tries to follow 2 to the baseline side of the screen, and if X3 stays with 3, then 2 can change directions and cut in front of the screen. Player 1 passes the ball to 2, who promptly makes a power move shot.

As 2 makes his cut, 3 can pop to the corner. Player 1 can pass the ball to 3 for a short jump shot.

Give-and-Go (2-1-2 Set)

Run the Play

Player 2 passes the ball to 5 in the high post.

Player 2 cuts toward the high post, and then cuts to the basket. Player 5 pivots to face the basket.

Scoring opportunity. Player 5 passes the ball to 2 for the layup.

Focus on Fundamentals

Player 5 should protect the ball in the high post, and pivot to face the basket.

Player 2's cut is similar to a V-cut since he first takes a short step in one direction before pushing off the plant foot to shift his momentum toward the basket. V-cuts, however, are used to cut *away* from the basket to receive a pass. In this case, 2 is cutting *to* the basket to receive the pass. The mechanics, however, are the same: 2 needs to bend his knees a bit to gather momentum for the explosive pushoff.

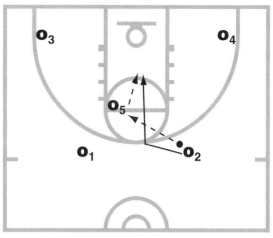

Give-and-go.

Defend the Play

The defense should be prepared to defend a scissor play (see Chapter 6) if 2 tries to cut to the opposite side of the screen set by 5 instead of cutting straight to the basket.

Players X3 and X4 need to help out as 2 cuts into the lane, but also keep an eye on 3 or 4 cutting to the basket along the baseline.

Second Options

If 2 cannot quickly cut to the basket on the ball side for the give-and-go, he can start a scissor play (see Basic Scissor, High Post Pass to Cutter on pages 54–56) by using a screen set by 5 to cut to the basket on the weak side.

Give-and-Go, Strong Side (1-3-1 Set)

Run the Play

Player 1 makes the entry pass to 2, then cuts to the high post.

Player 5 sets a screen for 1 so 1 can cut to the basket.

Scoring opportunity. Player 2 passes the ball to 1 for the layup.

Focus on Fundamentals

Spacing. Player 4 should clear out and go to the weak-side wing. Player 3 rotates up to assume the point guard position.

Give-and-go, strong side.

Player 5 should face 1 and set a strong screen for her. After 1 cuts through the screen, 5 turns to 2 with her hands up ready to receive a pass. Even though this play doesn't call for a pass from the wing into the high post, 5 should be ready for one. Also, by putting her hands up ready to receive a pass, 5 draws attention away from 1 cutting to the basket.

Defend the Play

Players X1 and X5 should communicate who will cover the screen cutter and who will cover the screener.

Player 4 should rotate out to try and draw X4 out of the lane and out of position so X4 can't help out. So X4 should keep an eye on 4, but also should provide help to defend against 1 or 5 cutting into the lane or 2 driving into the lane.

Second Options

Scoring opportunities. If X1 and X5 both cover 1 cutting into the lane, 5 can get open. In this case, 2 can pass the ball to 5 for a short jump shot.

After 1 cuts to the basket, 5 may also be in a position to cut (as a second cutter) to the basket for a pass from 2.

After 2 receives the entry pass, she may be in a triple threat position with the ball in a one-on-one situation. If weak-side help is not engaged, 2 may be able to execute a fake-out move (see pages 100–105) and drive to the basket.

Give-and-Go, Wing Cuts to Basket (1-2-2 Set)

Run the Play

Player 5 V-cuts to receive the pass from 2.

Player 2 cuts toward the lane and then cuts to the basket.

Scoring opportunity. Player 5 passes the ball to 2 for the layup.

Give-and-go, wing cuts to basket.

Focus on Fundamentals

Players 3 and 4 should always be moving, and can use any of the Get Open! Plays (refer back to pages 17–21) to free each other up. For example, 3 can down screen for 4, who can then use the screen to cut into the lane for a pass from 5.

Player 5 should make quick decisions from a triple threat position. If 5 dribbles merely for the sake of dribbling, 5 can easily dribble himself into the corner.

Defend the Play

The offense is quite spread out in this play. Players X3 and X4 should be in a good position to help out against the cutter.

Second Options

After 2 makes his cut, players 1, 3, or 4 can cut into the lane to receive a pass from 5. Player 2 can also baseline screen for 4, who can then cut into the lane for a pass from 5 for a power move basket.

Give-and-Go from Stack Set

Run the Play

Players 4 and 5 cut to the wing.

Players 2 and 3 cut to the high post.

Player 1 passes the ball to 5 (or 4), and then cuts to the basket.

Scoring opportunity. Player 5 passes the ball to 1 for the layup.

Focus on Fundamentals

If X2 is behind 2, then X2 may be on the passing line from 5 to 1. Player 5 may need to take a quick dribble or two to improve his passing angle to 1, or look for another option or play.

Players 3 and 4 (and 2 and 5) have to stack up closely. This lets each player use the other player as a kind of screen to free himself from his defender.

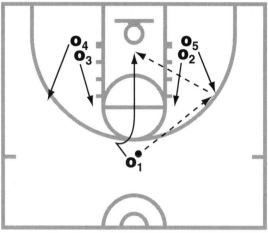

Give-and-go from stack set.

Defend the Play

Stack sets can cause unnecessary confusion among young defenses. Approach stack-set defense like you would screen defense. Your players should communicate who is covering whom.

Second Options

Scoring opportunity. By quickly popping out from the stack set, 5 has a very good chance to receive the pass for a *quick hitter* (a quick jump shot; see Chapter 11). If a quick hitter is not available, 5 should look for 1 cutting down the lane.

CHAPTER 4

Backdoor Plays

The classic backdoor situation arises when a player is being overplayed. Let's say the point guard is desperately trying to get an entry pass into the wing to begin a set play. But the player defending the wing player is *overplaying*—playing very close and aggressively denying the ball. Since many open jump shots are made from the wing, the wing defender may be overplaying to prevent a great jump-shooting wing player from getting the ball. Another reason for overplaying the wing is to prevent a low post play since many low post plays start with a pass from the wing. A pass made from the wing into the low post is less likely to be picked off than a pass from the point guard directly from the top of the key to the low post.

One strategy to get the ball into the wing is to use one of the Get Open! Plays (refer back to pages 17–21) to free up the wing using down screens or back screens. However, you can sometimes create an immediate scoring opportunity by using the defenders' zeal against them. All the wing player has to do is create just enough space between him and his defender and then bolt to the basket. He can do this by taking an initial step to the ball to draw his defender away from the basket. If the defender takes the bait, then the wing player immediately cuts behind the defender to the basket.

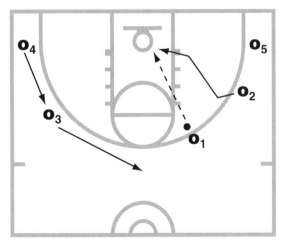

Basic backdoor.

Basic Backdoor (1-2-2 Set)

Run the Play

Player 1 fakes a pass to 2 at the wing.

Player 2 backdoor cuts to the basket.

Scoring opportunity. Player 1 passes the ball to 2 for the layup.

Focus on Fundamentals

Player 1 may need to take a quick dribble or two to improve her passing angle to 2.

Player 2 uses a backdoor cut to draw X2 away from the basket (in the diagram, toward 1) for just an instant, creating just enough space for 2 to bolt in the opposite direction toward the basket. A backdoor cut is similar to a V-cut in that 2 first takes a short step in one direction (in this case, away from the basket) before pushing off that foot to shift her momentum in another direction (in this case, toward the basket). Player 2 should bend her knees a bit to get momentum for the explosive pushoff.

Spacing. Player 4 should rotate to the wing as 2 cuts to the basket. This helps draw X4 out of position to help out. Player 3 can rotate to fill the open space at the top of the key.

Defend the Play

Player X2 should deny the ball by getting into a good defensive stance with one hand (the denial hand) and one foot in the passing line while keeping an eye on the ball and 2 at the same time. When 2 makes her backdoor cut, X2 should change direction by turning her head (over her other shoulder) and switching her denial hand.

Backdoor Pass from High Post (1-2-2 Set)

Run the Play

Players 2 and 3 break to the wing.

Player 1 passes to 5 in the high post.

Player 3 backdoor cuts to the basket.

Scoring opportunity. Player 5 passes the ball to 3 for the layup.

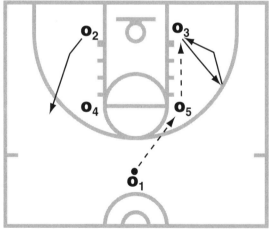

Focus on Fundamentals

Player 5 must protect the ball after he catches it, and pivot to face the basket so that he can make the pass to the 3, the cutter.

Defend the Play

Player X3 should deny the ball by getting into a good defensive stance with one hand (his denial hand) and one foot in the passing line while keeping an eye on the ball and 3 at the same time. When 3 makes his backdoor cut, X3 changes direction by turning his head (over his other shoulder) and switching his denial hand.

Backdoor pass from high post.

CHAPTER 5

Pick-and-Roll

A properly executed pick-and-roll is one of the most effective ways to use screens (picks) to create size mismatches. Typically, a forward (a 4, like Karl Malone) sets a wide-stance back screen for a guard (a 1, like John Stockton), who dribbles the ball toward the screen. If 1 is able to dribble close to the screen (shoulder to shoulder with 4), this will make it very difficult for X1 to follow 1 through the screen. This will force a switch, resulting in X1 having to guard the typically taller 4. Player 4 waits for 1 to finish using the screen, and then 4 rolls by pivoting and taking a drop step toward the basket. If 4 rolls to the basket with his hand up to give 1 a good target, then chances are good that 1 will be able to get a quick pass into the lane for 4 to make a layup or power move.

Basic pick-and-roll 1.

Basic Pick-and-Roll (2-1-2 Set)

Run the Play

Player 2 makes the entry pass to 1.

Player 4 back screens for 1 (the pick).

Player 1 dribbles off the screen to the basket.

Player 4 pivots and rolls to the basket (the roll).

Scoring opportunity. Player 1 passes the ball to 4 for the layup.

Focus on Fundamentals

A pick-and-roll works best when the play is executed in isolation (in this case, just 1 and 4 on the strong side). The idea is to keep the weak-side defenders busy so that they won't be in a good position to help out. For example, 3 and 5 can keep X3 and X5 occupied by down screening or back screening for each other. Remind your players (in this case, 1 and 4) to make sure not to place the screen too close to weak-side help. For example, if 4 sets the screen too close to the lane, then he'll end up rolling into traffic.

Player 1 should dribble shoulder to shoulder off the screen. Many young players have difficulty using screens and cutting shoulder to shoulder without the ball; cutting shoulder to shoulder while dribbling the ball with a defender playing on-ball defense can be even harder for them. One way to practice this skill is to have your players practice dribbling off stationary screens (set by a coach or a player).

Player 4 should find and then seal off X1 with a wide stance (feet wider than shoulders) and his hands up. Sealing off X1 forces the defenders to switch into a mismatch. A wide stance also allows 4 to roll to the basket with a large first step. Basketball is a contact sport, so 4's wide stance also helps him keep his balance when screen contact occurs. Having his hands up gives an immediate target for 1 to pass to as soon as 4 begins to roll.

Player 4 rolls by pivoting with the foot closest to the basket, and taking a drop step with his other foot. He should not step forward with his other foot. A big, aggressive drop step puts 4 in front of X1 on the switch, which helps get 4 to the basket quicker and puts him in a better position to block out for a rebound in case 1 decides to take a jump shot.

Player 4 should *wait* for 1 to brush by, and then promptly roll to the basket with his target hand up. If 4 rolls (leaves) before 1 has dribbled shoulder to shoulder, there is no need for the defenders to switch, meaning that X4 stays with 4 so there is no mismatch to take advantage of. Remind your 4 to take a big first drop step from a wide stance, and to make sure that his butt makes contact with the defender.

Because of the size mismatch on the switch, 1 may need to make a bounce pass to get the ball "under" X4 and on its way to the rolling 4. However, be aware that the smaller X1 may be in a better position to pick off a bounce pass than a pass lobbed over X1's head into the taller 4's outstretched hands.

Defend the Play

Pick-and-rolls work best when the defenders are forced to switch, causing a mismatch. When the defenders switch, the forward or center who rolls to the basket ends up being guarded by the typically smaller guard. In a mismatch, the forward or center usually has the advantage when attempting a layup or power move basket and when blocking out and rebounding a missed field goal attempt. Therefore, the best defensive strategy to counter a pick-and-roll is to try to beat the screen and to not switch. Communication, as always, is paramount in screen defense. The player guarding the screener (in this case, 4) has to alert the player defending the dribbler/screen cutter (in this case, 1) of the imminent screen.

Player X1 should use aggressive on-ball defense to pressure 1 to dribble away from the screen. However, if 1 is able to dribble close to the screen, then X1 should try to go over the screen, or fight over the screen, by taking a series of short explosive steps to follow 1 through the screen. We like the phrase *fight over the screen* because it is more accurate; it's not easy to try to go through a screen by getting between the screener and the screen cutter, both of whom are trying to squeeze out X1. As X1 quickly steps between the screener and screen cutter, he should stick his hips and torso out to help him fight his way through as he steps over the wide-leg stance of the screener. If X1 tries to defend the screen by going around it, instead of fighting over the screen, this generally leaves the ball handler open for the jump shot. Player X1 won't be able to directly see the screen coming, so he's allowed to put his hand out to help him find the screen. This is similar to how a softball player puts her hand out as she approaches the outfield wall while she's using her eyes to track down a fly ball.

If X1 can't fight over the screen, then X1 and X4 should switch. Player X4 switches by jumping in front of 1 as he dribbles, which is called a jump switch. Player X4's goal is to force 1 to change his plan—change direction or pick up his dribble and stop dead in his tracks. And if X4 can draw an offensive foul against 1, that's gravy. When the defenders switch, the rolling 4 will have a head start to the basket against X1. So by getting 1 to change his plan, X4 might be able to buy some time for X1 to catch up to 4 rolling to the basket, as well as for weak-side help to arrive. Or maybe 1 will get unnerved enough to abandon the pick-and-roll altogether.

Second Options

If the lane is wide open, and 4 doesn't or can't roll to the basket, this may be a good opportunity for 1 to drive to the basket using a fake-out move (see pages 100–105).

Scoring opportunity. If 4 doesn't or can't roll to the basket and remains stationary, 1 can use the screen to drive to the basket for a layup. If 4 rolls, and X1 and X4 mistakenly both go with 4, 1 can pull up for a short jump shot.

Basic pick-and-roll 2.

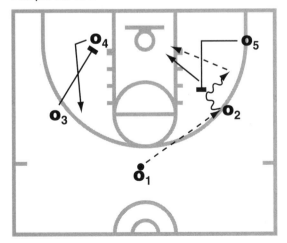

Basic Pick and Roll (1-2-2 Set)

Run the Play

Player 1 makes the entry pass to 2.

Player 5 back screens for 2 (the pick). Player 2 dribbles off the screen toward the corner.

Player 5 pivots and rolls to the basket (the roll).

Scoring opportunity. Player 2 passes the ball to 5 for the layup.

Focus on Fundamentals

Rather than going straight to the back screen, 5 should V-cut before setting the back screen. By V-cutting, 5 gives the impression that he is just trying to get open to receive the pass, which may delay weak-side help from arriving to help defend against the pick-and-roll.

A pick-and-roll works best when the play is executed in isolation (in this case, just 2 and 5 on the strong side). The idea is to keep the weak-side defenders busy so that they won't be in a good position to help out. For example, 3 and 4 can keep X3 and X4 occupied by down screening or back screening for each other. Remind your players to make sure not to place the screen too close to weak-side help. For example, if the screen is set too close to the lane, the player will end up rolling into traffic.

Player 2 should dribble shoulder to shoulder off the screen. Many young players have difficulty using screens and cutting shoulder to shoulder without the ball; cutting shoulder to shoulder while dribbling the ball with a defender playing on-ball defense can be even harder for them. One way to practice this skill is to have your players practice dribbling off stationary screens (set by a coach or a player).

Player 5 should find and then seal off X2 with a wide stance (feet wider than shoulders) and his hands up. Sealing off X2 forces the defenders to switch into a mismatch. A wide stance also allows 5 to roll to the basket with a large first step. Basketball is a contact sport, so 5's wide stance also helps him keep his balance when screen contact occurs. Having his hands up gives an immediate target for 2 to pass to as soon as 5 begins to roll.

Player 5 rolls by pivoting with the foot closest to the basket, and taking a drop step with his other foot. He should not step forward with his other foot. A big, aggressive drop step puts 5 in front of X2 on the switch, which helps get 5 to the basket quicker and puts 5 in a better position to block out for a rebound in case 2 decides to take a jump shot.

Player 5 should *wait* for 2 to brush by, and then promptly roll to the basket with his target hand up. If 5 rolls (leaves) before 2 has dribbled shoulder to shoulder, there is no need for the defenders to switch, meaning that X5 stays with 5 so there is no mismatch to take advantage of. Remind your 5 to take a big first drop step from a wide stance, and to make sure that his butt makes contact with the defender.

Because of the size mismatch on the switch, 2 may need to make a bounce pass to get the ball "under" X5 and on its way to the rolling 5. However, be aware that the smaller X2 may be in a better position to pick off a bounce pass than a pass lobbed over X2's head into the taller 5's outstretched hands.

Defend the Play

Pick-and-rolls work best when the defenders are forced to switch, causing a mismatch. When the defenders switch, the forward or center who rolls to the basket ends up being guarded by the typically smaller guard. In a mismatch, the forward or center usually has the advantage when attempting a layup or power move basket, and when blocking out and rebounding a missed field goal attempt. Therefore, the best defensive strategy to counter a pick-and-roll is to try to beat the screen and to not switch. Communication, as usual, is paramount in screen defense. The player guarding the screener has to alert the player defending the dribbler/screen cutter of the imminent screen.

Player X2 should use aggressive on-ball defense to pressure 2 to dribble away from the screen. However, if 2 is able to dribble close to the screen, then X2 should try to fight over the screen, by taking a series of short explosive steps to follow 2 through the screen. As X2 quickly steps between the screener and screen cutter, he should stick his hips and torso out to help him fight his way through as he steps over the wide-leg stance of the screener. If X2 tries to defend the screen by going around it, instead of fighting over the screen, this generally leaves the ball handler open for the jump shot. Player X2 won't be able to directly see the screen coming, so he's allowed to put his hand out to help him find the screen.

If X2 can't fight over the screen, then X2 and X5 should switch. Player X5 switches by jumping in front of 2 as he dribbles, which is called a jump switch. Player 5's goal is to force 2 to change his plan—change direction or pick up his dribble and stop dead in his tracks. And if X5 can draw an offensive foul against 2, that's gravy. When the defenders switch, the rolling 5 will have a head start to the basket against X2. So by getting 2 to change his plan, X5 might be able to buy some time for X2 to catch up to 5 rolling to the basket, as well as for weak-side help to arrive. Or maybe 2 will get unnerved enough to abandon the pick-and-roll altogether.

Second Options

If 1 can't make the entry pass to 2, then 1 can reverse the ball to 3. Player 3 can try to run a pick-and-roll with 4 setting the back screen for 3; that is, 4 picks, 3 dribbles, 4 rolls. Players 3 and 4 need to run the play quickly before weak-side help has a chance to react.

Scoring opportunity. After 1 makes the entry pass to 2, 1 can screen away for 3 on the weak side. Player 3 can use the screen to cut into the lane. If 2 determines that the pick-and-roll isn't going to work, then 2 can pass the ball to 3 cutting into the lane for a layup. Player 2 may need to dribble to improve his passing angle before passing to 3. Player 2 also has to be aware of X5, who is no longer defending the pick-and-roll and is available to help out against 3 coming into the lane from the weak side.

Pick-and-Roll with Low Post Stack (2-3 Set)

Run the Play

Players 3 and 5 set up in a low post stack on the block.

Player 3 breaks to the wing, and 1 passes the ball to 3.

At the same time, 5 V-cuts and then sets a back screen for 3 (the pick).

Player 3 dribbles off the screen toward the basket.

Player 5 pivots and rolls to the basket (the roll).

Scoring opportunity. Player 3 passes the ball to 5 for the layup.

Focus on Fundamentals

By V-cutting before setting the back screen, 5 gives the impression that he is just trying to get open to receive the pass, which may delay weak-side help from arriving to help defend against the pick-and-roll.

A pick-and-roll works best when the play is executed in isolation. The idea is to keep the weak-side defenders busy so that they won't be in a good position to help out. For example, 2 and 4 can keep X2 and X4 occupied by down screening or back screening for each other.

Player 3 should dribble shoulder to shoulder off the screen. Many young players have difficulty using screens and cutting shoulder to shoulder without the ball; cutting shoulder to shoulder while dribbling the ball with a defender playing on-ball defense can be even harder for them. One way to practice this skill is to have your players practice dribbling off stationary screens (set by a coach or a player).

Player 5 should find and then seal off X3 with a wide stance (feet wider than shoulders) and his hands up. Sealing off X3 forces the defenders to switch into a mismatch. A wide stance also allows 5 to roll to the basket with a large first step. Basketball is a contact sport, so 5's wide stance also helps him keep his balance when screen contact occurs. Having his hands up gives an immediate target for 3 to pass to as soon as 5 begins to roll.

Player 5 rolls by pivoting with the foot closest to the basket, and taking a drop step with his other foot. He should not step forward with his other foot. A big, aggressive drop step puts 5 in front of X3 on the switch, which helps get 5 to the basket quicker and puts 5 in a better position to block out for a rebound in case 3 decides to take a jump shot.

Player 5 should *wait* for 3 to brush by, and then promptly roll to the basket with his target hand up. If 5 rolls (leaves) before 3 has dribbled shoulder to shoulder, there is no need for the defenders to switch, meaning that X5 stays with 5 so there is no mismatch to take advantage of. Remind your 5 to take a big first drop step from a wide stance, and to make sure that his butt makes contact with the defender.

Because of the size mismatch on the switch, 3 may need to make a bounce pass to get the ball "under" X5 and on its way to the rolling 5. However, be aware that the smaller X3 may be in a better position to pick off a bounce pass than a pass lobbed over X3's head into the taller 5's out-stretched hands.

Defend the Play

Players X2 and X4 should be in weak-side help mode, but also be alert to 1 reversing the ball to the other side (see the Second Options section below).

Pick-and-rolls work best when the defenders are forced to switch, causing a mismatch. When the defenders switch, the forward or center who rolls to the basket ends up being guarded by the typically smaller guard. In a mismatch, the forward or center usually has the advantage when attempting a layup or power move basket, and when blocking out and rebounding a missed field goal attempt. Therefore, the best defensive strategy to counter a pick-and-roll is to try to beat the screen and to not switch. Communication, as usual, is paramount in screen defense. The player guarding the screener has to alert the player defending the dribbler/screen cutter of the imminent screen.

Player X3 should use aggressive on-ball defense to pressure 3 to dribble away from the screen. However, if 3 is able to dribble close to the screen, then X3 should try to fight over the screen, by taking a series of short explosive steps to follow 3 through the screen. As X3 quickly steps between the screener and screen cutter, he should stick his hips and torso out to help him fight his way through as he steps over the wide-leg stance of the screener. If X3 tries to defend the screen by going around it, instead of fighting over the screen, this generally leaves the ball handler open for the jump shot. Player X3 won't be able to directly see the screen coming, so he's allowed to put his hand out to help him find the screen.

If X3 can't fight over the screen, then X3 and X5 should switch. Player X5 switches by jumping in front of 3 as he dribbles, which is called a jump switch. Player 5's goal is to force 3 to change his plan—change direction or pick up his dribble and stop dead in his tracks. And if X5 can draw an offensive foul against 3, that's gravy. When the defenders switch, the rolling 5 will have a head start to the basket against X3. So by getting 3 to change his plan, X5 might be able to buy some time for X3 to catch up to 5 rolling to the basket, as well as for weak-side help to arrive. Or maybe 3 will get unnerved enough to abandon the pick-and-roll altogether.

Second Options

If 1 can't make the entry pass to 3, then 1 can reverse the ball to 2. Player 2 can try to run a pick-and-roll with 4 setting the back screen for 2; that is, 4 picks, 2 dribbles, 4 rolls. Players 4 and 2 need to run the play quickly before weak-side help has a chance to react.

Scoring opportunity. If 1 can't get the entry pass to 3, then 2 can down screen for 4 on the weak side. Player 4 can use the screen to cut into the lane. Player 1 may need to dribble to improve his passing angle before passing to 4 cutting into the lane for a layup.

Pick-and-Roll (1-4 Set)

Run the Play

Player 4 back screens for 1 (the pick).

Player 1 dribbles off the screen to the basket.

Player 4 pivots and rolls to the basket (the roll).

Scoring opportunity. Player 1 passes the ball to 4 for the layup.

Focus on Fundamentals

A pick-and-roll works best when the play is executed in isolation. The idea is to keep the weak-side defenders busy so that they won't be in a good position to help out. For example, 2, 3, and 5 can keep X3 and X5 occupied by continuously moving.

Player 1 should dribble shoulder to shoulder off the screen. Many young players have difficulty using screens and cutting shoulder to shoulder without the ball; cutting shoulder to shoulder while dribbling the ball with a defender playing on-ball defense can be even harder for them. One way to practice this skill is to have your players practice dribbling off stationary screens (set by a coach or a player).

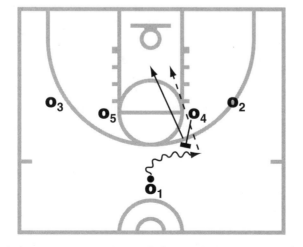

Pick-and-roll.

Player 4 should find and then seal off X1 with a wide stance (feet wider than shoulders) and his hands up. Sealing off X1 forces the defenders to switch into a mismatch. A wide stance also allows 4 to roll to the basket with a large first step. Basketball is a contact sport, so 4's wide stance also helps him keep his balance when screen contact occurs. Having his hands up gives an immediate target for 1 to pass to as soon as 4 begins to roll.

Player 4 rolls by pivoting with the foot closest to the basket, and taking a drop step with his other foot. He should not step forward with his other foot. A big, aggressive drop step puts 4 in front of X1 on the switch, which helps get 4 to the basket quicker and puts 4 in a better position to block out for a rebound in case 1 decides to take a jump shot.

Player 4 should *wait* for 1 to brush by, and then promptly roll to the basket with his target hand up. If 4 rolls (leaves) before 1 has dribbled shoulder to shoulder, there is no need for the defenders to switch, meaning that X4 stays with 4 so there is no mismatch to take advantage of. Remind your 4 to take a big first drop step from a wide stance, and to make sure that his butt makes contact with the defender.

Because of the size mismatch on the switch, 1 may need to make a bounce pass to get the ball "under" X4 and on its way to the rolling 4. However, be aware that the smaller X1 may be in a better position to pick off a bounce pass than a pass lobbed over X1's head into the taller 4's outstretched hands.

Defend the Play

Players X3 and X5 should get into weak-side help position as soon as 1 dribbles to the screen.

Your players should watch for 2 and 5 making backdoor cuts to the basket.

Pick-and-rolls work best when the defenders are forced to switch, causing a mismatch. When the defenders switch, the forward or center who rolls to the basket ends up being guarded by the typically smaller guard. In a mismatch, the forward or center usually has the advantage when attempting a layup or power move basket, and when blocking out and rebounding a missed field goal attempt. Therefore, the best defensive strategy to counter a pick-and-roll is to try to beat the screen and to not switch. Communication, as usual, is paramount in screen defense. The player guarding the screener has to alert the player defending the dribbler/screen cutter of the imminent screen.

Player X1 should use aggressive on-ball defense to pressure 1 to dribble away from the screen. However, if 1 is able to dribble close to the screen, then X1 should try to fight over the screen, by taking a series of short explosive steps to follow 1 through the screen. As X1 quickly steps between the screener and screen cutter, he should stick his hips and torso out to help him fight his way through as he steps over the wide-leg stance of the screener. If X1 tries to defend the screen by going around it, instead of fighting over the screen, this generally leaves the ball handler open for the jump shot. Player X1 won't be able to directly see the screen coming, so he's allowed to put his hand out to help him find the screen.

If X1 can't fight over the screen, then X1 and X4 should switch. Player X4 switches by jumping in front of 1 as he dribbles, which is called a jump switch. Player X4's goal is to force 1 to change his plan—change direction or pick up his dribble and stop dead in his tracks. And if X4 can draw an offensive foul against 1, that's gravy. When the defenders switch, the rolling 4 will have a head start to the basket against X1. So by getting 1 to change his plan, X4 might be able to buy some time for X1 to catch up to 4 rolling to the basket, as well as for weak-side help to arrive. Or maybe 1 will get unnerved enough to abandon the pick-and-roll altogether.

Second Options
Scoring opportunity. If X3 sags off to help out, 3 might be able to make a backdoor cut to the basket, or just drop back a few steps to receive the pass from 1 for a jump shot.

CHAPTER 6

Scissor Plays

Scissor plays are more advanced plays that involve two screen cutters splitting the high post on both sides. They work best for teams with strong, savvy post players who are able to protect the ball in dense traffic and can read and exploit defensive lapses by executing any number of variations. Scissor plays may be somewhat confusing for younger players, so teach them the basic version after they have mastered some of the other plays in this book that use screens (such as the Pass and Screen Away on page 32 and the basic baseline screens in Chapter 7).

Basic Scissor, High Post Pass to Cutter (2-1-2 Set)

Run the Play
Player 1 passes the ball to 5 in the high post or pivot area.

Player 5 protects the ball and sets a screen.

Player 1 cuts to the ball, and screens off 5 to the basket.

Player 2 cuts to the ball, and screens off 5 to the basket.

Scoring opportunity. Player 5 pivots to face the basket and passes to 1 or 2 for the layup.

Focus on Fundamentals
Player 5 should catch the pass from 1 by jumping to the ball with both feet off the ground and landing on both feet simultaneously. This ensures that 5 can use either foot as the pivot foot as necessary. She should protect the ball by holding it with both hands near her chin with her elbows out.

Players 1 and 2 split the post, but the player who passes to 5 in the pivot is the first cutter.

The second cutter (2) waits for the first cutter (1) to cut off the screen. Then the 2 cutter cuts off the screen. They should both cut shoulder to shoulder off the strong screen set by 5.

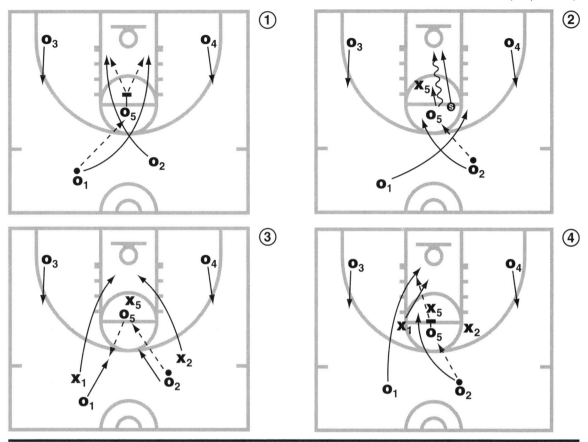

Basic scissor, high post pass to cutter. ① Player 1 passes to 5. ② Options for 5 in the high post—5 takes it to the hole. ③ Players 1 and 2 fake the scissor cut. ④ Player 1 abandons the scissor cut and cuts straight to the basket.

Both 1 and 2 should fake in the opposite direction before heading for the screen. Players 3 and 4 should keep moving.

Defend the Play
Players X1 and X2 should use quick feet to pressure 1 and 2 away from the screen set by 5. This will give X1 and X2 a chance to follow 1 and 2 through the screen.

Players X1, X2, or X5 can try to prevent 1 (or 2) from making her scissor cut by stepping in her path. However, if the defenders try this tactic, they should be prepared for 5 pivoting and drop-stepping for a drive to the basket, or a quick return pass from 5 to 1 (or 2). In turn, 1 or 2, instead of making a scissor cut, can pop back to the top of the key to receive a pass for a jump shot (although this would literally be a long shot for some younger players). See also the Second Options section below.

Second Options

After 5 receives the ball in the pivot area, if X5 tries to prevent 1 from making her scissor cut by stepping in 1's path, 5 can pivot with her left foot, and take a drop step with her right foot toward the basket. This assumes, of course, that 5 has the option to pivot with that foot (the best way to keep her pivot options open is to catch the pass from 1 by jumping to it and landing on both feet simultaneously). Player 5 should make sure that her butt makes contact with X5 as she pivots and takes the drop step. By doing this, 5 will have sealed X5 behind her, and 5 can then take the ball to the hole by herself. If other defenders are helping out in the lane, 5 may need to pull up for a short jump shot (diagram 2 on page 55).

If 3 or 4 is able to get in front of her defender, then 5 can look to pass the ball down to the low post. Players 3 and 4 may need to set baseline screens for each other in order to free up one of them for a pass from 5.

Players 1 and 2 need to be alert and adapt to how the defense reacts. If after 5 receives the ball in the pivot area, either X1 or X2 tries to anticipate the scissor cut by stepping behind X5, then 1 or 2 can fake but then not make the scissor cut and be open momentarily above the free throw line. Player 5 can promptly pass the ball to 1 or 2 (whoever is open) for a quick jump shot (diagram 3 on page 55). On the other hand if after 5 receives the ball, X1 anticipates by stepping in to prevent 2 from making her scissor cut, or X2 anticipates by stepping in to prevent 1 from making her scissor cut, then 1 or 2 can abandon the scissor cut and cut straight to the basket. Even in this case, 1 or 2 should cut shoulder to shoulder off of X5. Player 5 pivots and then passes the ball to either 1 or 2 (whoever is open) for the layup (diagram 4 on page 55).

On any of these plays, remind your players that after 1 (or 2) receives the pass from 5, if X3 or X4 sags off 3 or 4 to help defend the lane, then 1 (or 2) can pass the ball to 3 or 4 for a short jump shot.

Basic scissor, low post pass to cutter.

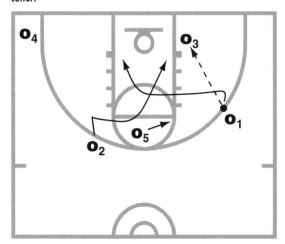

Basic Scissor, Low Post Pass to Cutter (2-1-2 Set)

Run the Play

Player 5 moves to the pivot to receive the pass from 1.

Instead, 1 passes the ball to 3 in the low post.

Player 1 cuts across the lane and then to the basket. At the same time, 2 cuts to the basket.

Players 1 and 2 coordinate their cuts to make X1 and X2 bump into each other.

Scoring opportunity. Player 3 passes to 1 or 2 for the layup.

Focus on Fundamentals

Timing is crucial because there is no stationary screen to work off of. Instead 1 and 2 must coordinate their movements to make X1 and X2 bump into each other.

Players 1 and 2 should fake a cut in another direction before cutting to the basket.

Defend the Play

Players X1 and X2 need to communicate whether each defender will defend his assigned player, or switch.

Second Options

When 3 receives the ball in the low post, he should look to make a low post move.

Scissor Handoff

Run the Play

Player 1 passes the ball to 5 in the high post.

Player 5 protects the ball and sets a screen.

Players 1 and then 2 initiate their scissor cuts, using the screen set by 5.

Scoring opportunity. Player 1 or 2 grabs the ball from 5 and drives to the basket for a layup.

Focus on Fundamentals

A handoff is always better than a sudden short pass, which can easily be fumbled.

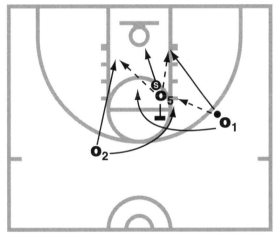

Scissor handoff.

Player 5 should catch the pass from 1 by jumping to the ball with both feet off the ground and landing on both feet simultaneously. This ensures that he can use either foot as the pivot foot if the handoff doesn't take place and he still has the ball. This gives 5 the most flexibility when trying to score (see the Second Options section below). Since 5 may be facing 1 when he lands with the ball, player 5 should brace himself for the screen and handoff, keeping in mind that 2 is cutting to 5 from 5's blind spot.

Defend the Play

Players X1 and X2 should use quick feet to pressure 1 and 2 away from the screen set by 5. This will give X1 and X2 a chance to follow 1 and 2 through the screen.

Players X1, X2, or X5 can try to prevent 1 (or 2) from making her scissor cut by stepping in her path. However, if the defenders try this tactic, they should be prepared for 5 pivoting and drop-stepping for a drive to the basket, or a quick return pass from 5 to 1 (or 2).

Second Options

Scoring opportunities. If the handoff is not an option, 5 should pivot to face the basket and pass to 1 or 2 (whoever is open) cutting to the basket.

Or 5 can drive to the basket or take a jump shot. He can use a fake-out move (see pages 100–105) to shake off or seal off his defender before driving or shooting.

Scissor with Wing Pass to Cutter (2-1-2 Set)

Run the Play

Player 1 makes the entry pass to 3.

Players 1 and then 2 initiate their scissor cuts, using the screen set by 5.

Scoring opportunity. Player 3 passes the ball to 2 for the layup.

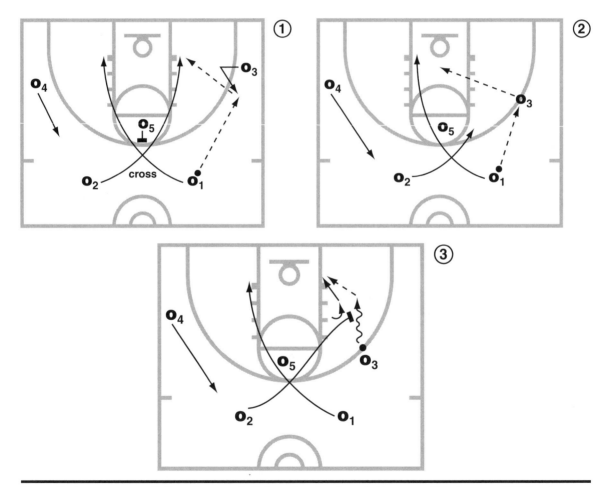

Scissor with wing pass to cutter. ① Player 1 passes to 3. ② A pass from 3 to the weak-side cutter could be dangerous. ③ With a size mismatch on the strong side, 2 and 3 can run a pick-and-roll.

Focus on Fundamentals

Player 3 should V-cut to try and get open for the entry pass. Player 1 may have to take a quick dribble or two to improve his passing angle to 3.

In a regular scissor play (such as a pass to the scissor cutters from the pivot area), the passer in the pivot area (usually 5) has a good passing angle to either cutter. However, in this play, the wing player (3) is making the pass. The only viable pass from the wing is a pass to the second cutter (in this case, 2)—the scissor cutter cutting to the strong side. The first scissor cutter (1) is cutting to the weak side, and the wing player would have to make a dangerous long-distance pass across the lane (diagram 2).

Spacing. Player 4 pops out to fill in the space formerly occupied by 2 (3 can pass the ball to 4 to start another set play if 2 is not open). The first scissor cutter (1) should make sure to clear the lane to draw the weak-side helpers out of the lane.

Defend the Play

Players X1 and X2 should use quick feet to pressure 1 and 2 away from the screen set by 5. This will give X1 and X2 a chance to follow 1 and 2 through the screen.

Players X1, X2, or X5 can try to prevent 1 (or 2) from making his scissor cut by stepping in his path. However, if the defenders try this tactic, they should be prepared for 5 pivoting and drop-stepping for a drive to the basket, or a quick return pass from 5 to 1 (or 2).

Second Options

Scoring opportunity. After 3 receives the entry pass on the wing, if X3 sags off 3 to help cover 1 (who is cutting to the pivot area), then 3 will momentarily be open to take a jump shot.

Let's say that 1 makes the entry pass to 3 and makes his scissor cut. Player 2 makes his scissor cut, but doesn't get the pass. So 3 still has the ball on the wing. If 1, 4, and 5 are on the weak side, and if there's a size mismatch on the strong side, then this may be a good opportunity for 2 and 3 to run a pick-and-roll (diagram 3).

CHAPTER 7

Baseline Screen Plays

Baseline screens are screens set near the blocks along the baseline. They generally are used by players to get free to take jump shots. If the player who uses the screen (the screen cutter) isn't able to get the shot off immediately, he can reverse direction and dribble the ball and use another screen set by the screener to drive to the basket, or pass the ball to the screener who is now set up to receive the ball in the low post.

Baseline Screen for Wing (1-2-2 Set)

Run the Play

Player 5 baseline screens for 2.

Player 2 passes to 1, cuts across the lane, and uses the screen to go to the corner.

Player 1 passes the ball to 3 who V-cuts to get open to receive the pass.

Scoring opportunity. Player 3 dribbles and passes the ball to 2 for the jump shot.

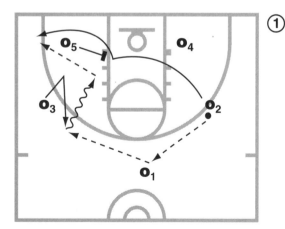

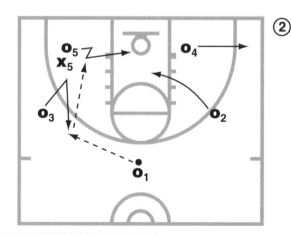

Baseline screen for wing 1. ① Player 5 baseline screens for 2. ② Player 5 V-cuts and then makes a backdoor cut to the basket.

Focus on Fundamentals

Player 2 can use a fake-out move away from the lane, and then make a backdoor cut to the basket.

After 2 receives the pass he should get into a triple threat position to give him the most flexibility in case he can't get the jump shot off immediately. He should dribble only when he is sure he won't be forced to pick up his dribble, especially since 2 is vulnerable to traps in the corner.

Player 5 should not set the screen too close to the baseline. Most defenders won't fight over the screen by following the screen cutter out-of-bounds (the screen cutter can't do too much damage from out-of-bounds). In most cases, they won't switch either; rather, they'll just wait for the screen cutter to return to the inbounds side of the court and resume coverage.

Player 1 can fake the entry pass to the opposite wing (2) and then pass to 3. Player 5 can V-cut as though he will receive a pass from 3. There are two movements in a V-cut—the first movement toward the basket and the second movement out to receive the pass. If the defender anticipates a V-cut, then the player executing the V-cut can just resume his first movement and make a backdoor cut to the basket (diagram 2).

This play can also be used to free up 4 for a jump shot (see Baseline Screen for Opposite Corner, pages 63–64). If the play is being used to free up the wing player, then 4 should pop out to the wing position formerly occupied by 2.

Defend the Play

Players X2 and X5 need to communicate who will cover the screen cutter (2) and who will cover the screener (5).

Players X2 and X5 should be aware of possible backdoor cuts by 2 or 5.

The defenders should be on the lookout for trapping opportunities in the corner.

Second Options

Scoring opportunities. If X2 and X5 switch, there may be a size mismatch. If 2 can't make the jump shot, 2 can pass the ball to 5 in the low post, and 5 can use his size advantage to make a low post move for a layup or a power move basket.

Player 3 should be on the watch for backdoor cuts by 2 or 5.

Baseline Screen for Wing (1-3-1 Set)

Run the Play

Player 4 baseline screens for 3.

Meantime, 1 makes the entry pass to 2.

Player 3 cuts across the lane, and uses the screen to go to the corner.

Scoring opportunity. Player 2 passes the ball to 3 for the jump shot.

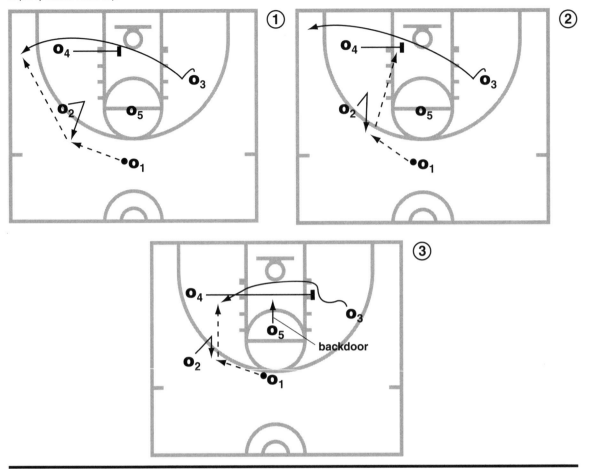

Baseline screen for wing 2. ① Player 4 baseline screens for 3. ② Player 2 passes to 4 in the low post. ③ Player 3 uses the screen to execute a low post move.

Focus on Fundamentals

Player 2 on the wing should V-cut to get open to receive the entry pass from 1. She should jump to the ball to receive the entry pass on the wing with both feet off the ground and land on both feet simultaneously. This allows 2 to choose a pivot foot. From her triple threat position, 2 can shoot, drive, or pass. As 3 makes her cut and clears the lane to the corner, she keeps her lead hand up to give 2 a passing target in case of an immediate backdoor opportunity. As 3 makes her cut, 2 may be able to drive to the basket, using a fake-out move to shake off her defender, if necessary, as well as another screen set by 4. Even if 2 doesn't drive, she may still need to take a dribble or two to improve her passing angle to 3 in the corner.

Defend the Play

Players X3 and X4 need to communicate who will cover the screen cutter (3) and who will cover the screener (4).

Player X4 should be alert to a possible backdoor cut by 4.

Second Options

Scoring opportunities. If X3 and X4 switch, there may be a size mismatch. If 3 can't shoot the jump shot, then 2 can pass the ball to 4 in the low post (diagram 2). Player 4 can use her size advantage to make a low post move for a layup or a power move basket.

Player 3 should be alert to a backdoor cut by 5.

If 4 sets the baseline screen on the opposite block, then 3 can use the screen to cut into the lane to receive a pass to execute a low post move for a jump hook basket (diagram 3). Player 4 should be aware that X5 may be in the lane to help out.

Baseline Screen for Opposite Corner (1-2-2 Set)

Run the Play

Player 5 baseline screens for 4.

Player 1 makes the entry pass to 3.

Player 4 cuts across the lane and uses the screen to go to the corner.

Scoring opportunity. Player 3 passes the ball to 4 for the jump shot.

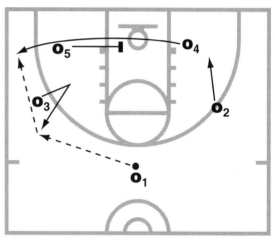

Baseline screen for opposite corner.

Focus on Fundamentals

After 4 receives the pass he should get into a triple threat position to give him the most flexibility in case he can't get the jump shot off immediately. He should dribble only when he is sure he won't be forced to pick up his dribble, especially since 4 is vulnerable to traps in the corner.

Player 5 should not set the screen too close to the baseline. Most defenders won't fight over the screen by following the screen cutter out-of-bounds (the screen cutter can't do too much damage from out-of-bounds). In most cases, they won't switch, either; rather, they'll just wait for the screen cutter to return to the inbounds side of the court and resume coverage.

Player 5 should be aware of the how much time he spends in the paint to avoid a 3-second violation. After 4 uses the screen, 5 can post up if X4 and X5 switch, leaving a smaller defender to cover 5, or 5 can clear out to the weak side, which will allow 4 to drive to the basket instead of taking the jump shot.

Defend the Play

Players X4 and X5 need to communicate who will cover the screen cutter (4) and who will cover the screener (5).

Player X5 should be alert to a possible backdoor cut by 5.

Second Options

Player 4 can pass the ball to 5 for a low post move to the basket.

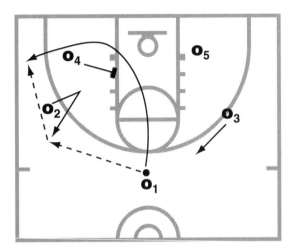

Baseline screen for point guard 1.

Baseline Screen for Point Guard (1-2-2 Set)

Run the Play

Player 4 baseline screens for 1.

Meantime, 1 makes the entry pass to 2.

Player 1 uses the screen to cut to the corner.

Scoring opportunity. Player 2 passes the ball to 1 for the jump shot.

Focus on Fundamentals

Player 2 on the wing should V-cut to get open to receive the entry pass from 1. She should jump to the ball to receive the entry pass on the wing with both feet off the ground and land on both feet simultaneously. This allows 2 to choose a pivot foot. From her triple threat position, 2 can shoot, drive, or pass. As 1 makes her cut and clears the lane to the corner, she keeps her lead hand up to give 2 a passing target in case of an immediate give-and-go opportunity. As 1 makes her cut, 2 may be able to drive to the basket, using a fake-out move to shake off her defender, if necessary, as well as another screen set by 4. Even if 2 doesn't drive, she may still need to take a dribble or two to improve her passing angle to 1 in the corner.

Defend the Play

Players X1 and X4 need to communicate who will cover the screen cutter (1) and who will cover the screener (4).

Player X4 should be alert to a possible backdoor cut by 4.

Second Options

Player 1 can pass the ball to 4 for a low post move to the basket, especially if X1 and X4 switch, leaving the smaller defender to cover 4 on the block.

Baseline Screen for Point Guard (2-1-2 Set)

Run the Play

Player 1 passes the ball to 2.

Player 5 sets a screen for 1 in the high post area.

Player 4 baseline screens for 1.

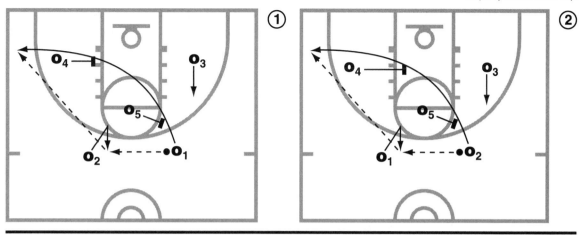

Baseline screen for point guard 2. ① Player 1 passes to 2. ② Player 2 is the outside shooter.

Player 1 cuts across the lane and uses the screen to go to the corner.
Scoring opportunity. Player 2 passes the ball to 1 for the jump shot.

Note that if 2 is your better outside shooter, you can also run the play for 2 (diagram 2).

Focus on Fundamentals

Player 2 on the wing should V-cut to get open to receive the entry pass from 1. He should jump to the ball to receive the entry pass on the wing with both feet off the ground and land on both feet simultaneously. This allows 2 to choose a pivot foot. From his triple threat position, 2 can shoot, drive, or pass. As 1 makes his cut and clears the lane to the corner, he keeps his lead hand up to give 2 a passing target in case of an immediate give-and-go opportunity. As 1 makes his cut, 2 may be able to drive to the basket, using a fake-out move to shake off his defender, if necessary, as well as another screen set by 4. Even if 2 doesn't drive, he may still need to take a dribble or two to improve his passing angle to 1 in the corner.

Defend the Play

The defenders need to communicate who will cover the screen cutter (1) and who will cover the screeners (4 and 5).

Players X4 and X5 should be alert to possible backdoor cuts by 4 or 5.

Second Options

Player 1 can pass the ball to 4 for a low post move to the basket, especially if X1 and X4 switch, leaving the smaller defender to cover 4 on the block. If the defender covering 1 converges and helps defend the low post, then 1 will be open again for the jump shot.

If 1 is not open, 2 can look to pass the ball to 5 in the high post to exploit any mismatch if X1 and X5 switch, leaving the smaller defender to cover 5.

Baseline Screen for Forward (2-3 Set)

Run the Play

Players 3 and 5 baseline screen for 4.

Meantime, 1 passes the ball to 2.

Player 4 uses the screens to cut across the lane to the opposite corner.

Scoring opportunity. Player 2 passes the ball to 4 for the jump shot.

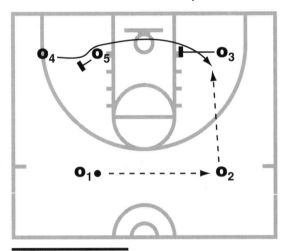

Baseline screen for forward.

Focus on Fundamentals

Player 2 should look for a defensive breakdown down low as 4 screens off 5 and 3, and a possible pass to either 3 or 5.

Defend the Play

The defenders need to communicate who will cover the screen cutter (4) and who will cover the screeners (3 and 5).

Player X3 should be alert to a possible backdoor cut by 3.

CHAPTER 8

Low Post Plays

A *low post play* is any play that involves a pass to a *post player* (any offensive player in a mismatch, but typically a center or forward) positioned within close range of the basket (on the block). Often, but not always, a low post player has his back to the basket. The defender (post defender) may be playing behind or in front. The post player uses a variety of techniques to seal out the post defender, receive the pass, and make an inside shot. These individual player techniques are discussed in Part Two.

Basic Low Post, Defender Behind (1-2-2 Set)

Run the Play
Player 4 is in front of X4 in the low post.

Player 1 makes the entry pass to 2.

Player 2 passes the ball to 4.

Scoring opportunity. Player 4 makes a low post move for the basket.

Focus on Fundamentals
Spacing. Player 5 should take care not to go into the lane. Otherwise X5 will be in a good position to help defend against 4's low post move.

Player 2 may need to take a quick dribble or two to improve his passing angle to 4.

In this play, X4 is already behind 4. Player 4

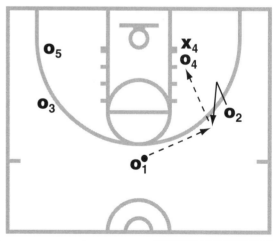

Basic low post, defender behind.

should use his hips (not his arms or hands) and a wide stance to push back, seal out, and keep X4 behind him to create a bigger passing area. Then, 4 tries to get square to the path of the pass from 2 with his hands up to give 2 a target.

Player 4 should try to catch the ball with both feet in the air, and make a jump stop to give him the option to use either foot as the pivot foot. He should receive the pass with his elbows out and with the ball under his chin to protect it.

If 4 is now closer to the basket compared to X4 as a result of using a low post move to shoot the ball, 4 should block out X4 and go for the offensive rebound.

Defend the Play

Player X4 jostles to get in front of 4 to deny the pass. If 4 is able to receive the pass and make a low post move and shoot the ball, X4 should block out and go for the defensive rebound.

Player X5 may be in a good position to help defend against 4, and to get possession of a poorly thrown lob pass from 2 to 4.

Second Options

Scoring opportunity. After passing the ball to 4 in the low post, 2 can break to the corner, and 4 can pass the ball to 2 for the jump shot.

Basic Low Post, Defender in Front (1-2-2 Set)

Run the Play

Player 1 makes the entry pass to 2.

Player 2 V-cuts to receive the ball and passes it to 4.

Scoring opportunity. Player 4 makes a low post move to the basket.

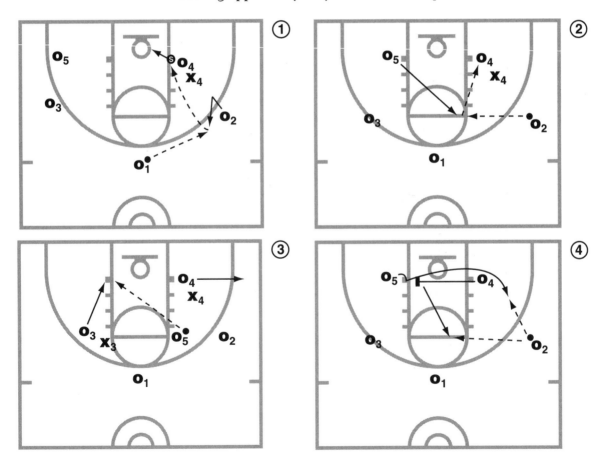

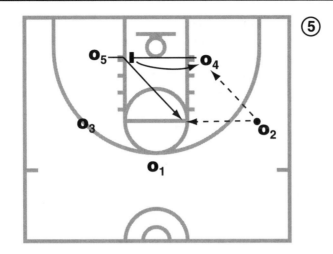

⑤

Basic low post, defender in front. ① Player 1 passes to 2. ② Player 5 receives the pass from 2 and passes to 4 in the low post. ③ Player 3 makes a backdoor cut to receive the pass from 5. ④ Player 2 passes to 5. ⑤ Player 2 can pass to 4 or 5.

Focus on Fundamentals

Player X4 is fronting 4 in the low post. Player 4 should use his hips (not his arms or hands) and a wide stance to push his defender forward (away from the basket) and toward the passer (2) to maintain inside position and create a bigger passing area for a possible overhead lob pass.

Player 2 may need to take a quick dribble or two to improve his passing angle to 4. After using his hips to keep X4 away from the basket, 4 can step toward the basket to receive a lob pass from 2. Player 2 can't make a bounce pass to 4 because X4 is fronting.

Since X4 is fronting, 4 is already closer to the basket compared to X4. Player 4 is in a good position to block out and go for an offensive rebound.

Defend the Play

Player X4 should deny the pass, but at the same time be alert to an overhead lob pass to 4.

Player X3 or X5 may be in a good position to help defend against an overthrown overhead lob pass.

The wing usually has the best passing angle into the low post, so one way to help prevent or delay a low post play from beginning is to play aggressive denial defense against the wing player (in this case, 2). Aggressive denial defense sometimes induces backdoor cuts, so X2 should be ready for this as well.

If 2 receives the ball on the wing and then passes the ball to 5 in the pivot area, the defenders should be ready for a scissor play (see Chapter 6) or any play where players use the pivot player as a screener.

Second Options

Scoring opportunities. If 4 is not open in the low post, 5 or 3 can pop out to the high post to receive a quick pass from 2, and either take a jump shot or try to pass the ball to 4 in the low post (diagram 2). Because X4 is fronting 4 in the low post, 5 or 3 in the high post may have a better passing angle than 2 into the low post. Also, if 5 is the player who pops out, then 3 can make a back-door cut to the basket for a pass from 5 for the layup (diagram 3 on page 68).

If 4 is not open in the low post, 4 can baseline screen for 5. Player 5 uses the screen to cut to either the strong-side block or into the lane. Meantime, after setting the screen, 4 can pop out to the high post. Player 2 can pass the ball to 5 for a power move basket, jump hook, or short jump shot (diagram 4 on page 68), or to 4 for a jump shot.

If 4 is not open in the low post, 4 can baseline screen for 5. Player 5 uses the screen to pop out to the high post to receive a pass from 2. Meantime, after setting the screen, 4 cuts to the strong-side block. Player 2 can pass the ball either to 5 for a jump shot, or to 4 for a power move basket (diagram 5 on page 69).

Low Post with Down Screen (1-2-2 Set)

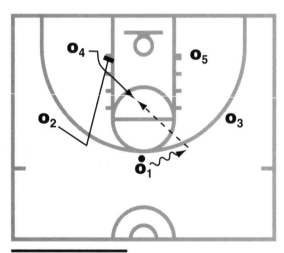

Low post with down screen.

Run the Play
Player 2 down screens for 4.

Player 4 uses the screen to cut into the lane.

Scoring opportunity. Player 1 passes the ball to 4, who pivots and squares up for the short jump shot or makes a power move basket.

Focus on Fundamentals
Player 2 should use her lower body to push her defender (X2 or X4, depending on whether the defenders switch) away from the basket and toward the baseline.

Player 1 may need to take a quick dribble or two to improve her passing angle to 4.

Defend the Play
Players X2 and X4 should communicate who will cover the screen cutter and who will cover the screener.

Second Options
Scoring opportunities. If 4 is not open, 2, who has sealed off the defender, may be open for a pass into the low post. Player 1 passes the ball (with a lob or bounce pass) to 2 for the power move basket. If the defenders have switched, and 2 is up against a taller X4, then 2 can try to make a jump hook shot, which will allow 2 to use the side of her body closest to the basket as a buffer zone.

Alternatively, after 2 has sealed off the defender, 2 can quickly pop to the wing for a pass from 1 and take a jump shot.

Backdoor with Back Screen (1-2-2 Set)

Run the Play

Player 4 back screens for 2.

Player 2 uses the screen to make a back-door cut to the basket.

Scoring opportunity. Player 1 passes the ball to 2 for the layup or power move basket.

Focus on Fundamentals

Player 4 should pivot to face the basket and use his lower body to push his defender (X2 or X4, depending on whether the defenders switch) away from the basket.

Defend the Play

Players X2 and X4 should communicate who will cover the screen cutter and who will cover the screener.

Second Options

Scoring opportunity. If 2 is not open, 2 clears the lane. Player 4, who has used his hips and lower body to push his defender away from the basket, can then take off for the basket. Player 4 keeps his hand up to give 1 a target to pass to. Player 1 passes the ball to 4 for the layup.

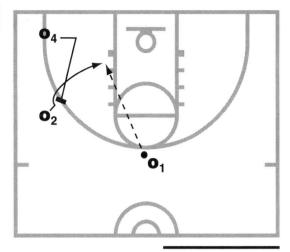

Backdoor with back screen.

Fast Breaks and Beating the Press

If only one team was allowed to put five players on the floor, the short-handed team would be at a tremendous disadvantage. While regulation basketball requires five players from each team to be on the floor at all times, a team that likes to run can create these types of mismatches by running *fast breaks*, plays in which a team gains possession of the ball (through a defensive rebound, steal, or made shot) and then pushes the ball toward the other basket as fast as possible, hoping to catch the other team off guard and score an easy shot. Common fast-break scenarios include *2-on-1* (two offensive players versus one defensive player) and *3-on-2* (three offensive players versus two defensive players). Unlike the set plays discussed earlier, which are executed entirely on the offensive side of the floor (the frontcourt), fast breaks are designed to move the ball very quickly from the defensive zone (the backcourt) into the offensive zone after a turnover by the other side. Very fast teams with good endurance use them as up-tempo strategies to move the ball down the court before the other team has a chance to set up its defense. Well-executed fast breaks typically result in uncontested layups or a trip to the foul line, if a defender has been able to get down the floor and commits a desperate or foolish foul.

One way to run a fast-break offense is to have any player who rebounds the ball become a point guard and quickly dribble the ball upcourt. This is another reason for you to develop dribbling skills in *all* your players (which you should be doing anyway). All the other players should sprint wide down the court and cut to the basket. Sometimes it's good to have one of the players be the *trailer*, who follows the designated point guard. If there are no opportunities in front of the point guard (he can't drive to the basket or pass it to one of the fast-break cutters) or if the point guard is in trouble (he picked up his dribble with nowhere to go and no one to pass to), then he can pass the ball to the trailer.

An offensive team has 10 seconds to move the ball from the backcourt to the frontcourt. If the opposing team figures out that your guards are weak or nervous ball handlers, it may decide to execute a *full-court press*, a man-to-man or zone defense in which the defensive players guard the other team starting while the other team still has possession of the ball in the backcourt before crossing midcourt. Teams use this to overplay the ball handlers (either by employing super-aggressive one-on-one on-ball defense or by double-teaming the ball) and deny passes in order to prevent the ball from crossing the midcourt line in time. Offenses should know how to beat the press, and we've included a play to help you do that. The most effective press, of course, is to prevent the ball from being inbounded in the first place (the team has 5 seconds to inbound), and we'll cover some basic inbounds plays to help you free up a player to receive the inbounds pass in Chapter 10.

Fast Break with Layup

Run the Play

Player 4 (or any player who has grabbed a defensive rebound) quickly dribbles the ball upcourt.

The other players sprint wide upcourt. The last player is the trailer.

At around the foul line extended, 4 either drives to the basket or passes the ball to a teammate cutting to the basket for a layup.

Focus on Fundamentals

The ball handler (in this case, 4) always keeps her options open—either to drive directly to the basket, to pass the ball to a player cutting to the basket, or to pass to the trailer, who is likely to be open as most defenders sprint toward the basket. She should never pick up her dribble unless she is sure she will be shooting or passing the ball.

If the ball handler decides to pass the ball to a player cutting to the basket, she'll have to make the pass so that the cutter can catch the ball without slowing down. The cutter should put her hand out to give the ball handler a target to pass to.

All cutters should sprint up the court. A cutter should not assume that she will not receive the ball—if she does and slows down as a result, that will telegraph the play to the defense.

Defend the Play

When a player takes a shot, her teammates should try to get the offensive rebound. However, at least one guard should stay back beyond the 3-point arc, ready to sprint down the court to help prevent a fast break by the other

Fast break with layup.

team in case they grab the defensive rebound. If the other team does grab the defensive rebound, the defender guarding the rebounder should play aggressive on-ball defense to block the outlet pass. Keep in mind that teams that like to run the fast break might have the rebounder dribble the ball up the court.

If two guards are playing back instead of one, the guard on the strong side should defend against the ball handler, and the other guard should sprint to the defensive end to try and prevent an easy basket. All the other defenders should sprint down the court. Defenders should never casually backpedal down the court on defense. Keep in mind that players can never run as fast backward as they can forward. Plus, backpedaling can be dangerous because the player is not looking where she is running.

Generally, the first responders (the fastest defenders) should go to the defensive lane area to protect against an easy basket. When the other defenders have caught up (5-on-5 situation), then the defenders can go out to guard their assigned opponents.

In a 5-on-5 situation, the defender guarding the ball should sprint, rather than slide or side-shuffle, to catch up and get between the ball handler and the basket. She should play good on-ball defense, including trying to force a right-handed player to dribble to her left (and presumably weaker) side, and vice versa. However, if the defense is outmanned on a fast break, the first priority is to *defend the basket*—prevent the player closest to the basket from getting the ball and scoring an easy basket. In a 2-on-1 fast break this may mean that the defensive player may need to concede a jump shot by the ball handler, but that's usually better than overplaying the ball handler and leaving another player open under the basket for a quick pass and then an easy uncontested layup. If there's help in the form of at least one more defender in the paint (say, in a 3-plus-on-2 fast break—that is, three or more offensive players versus two defensive players), then the defense has the luxury of having one defender challenge the ball handler. But even in this situation, the remaining defender should defend the basket, committing only when a cutter close to the basket has received the ball. Communication among the defenders is key because the defense should try not to leave any opponent open under the basket.

Fast Break with Rebound and Outlet

Run the Play

Player 4 (or any player who has grabbed a defensive rebound) makes an outlet pass to a ball handler (in this case, 1), who quickly dribbles the ball upcourt.

The other players sprint wide upcourt. The last player (in this case, the rebounder 4) is the trailer.

At around the foul line extended, 1 either drives to the basket, passes the ball to a teammate cutting to the basket for a layup, or to slow things down, passes back to the trailer.

Focus on Fundamentals

After grabbing the defensive rebound, the rebounder (in this case, 4) should land on both feet and protect the ball by tucking it near his chin with his elbows out. He then pivots away from any defenders and makes the outlet pass to a guard (in this case, 1).

The ball handler (1) always keeps his options open—either to drive directly to the basket or to pass the ball to a player cutting to the basket. He should never pick up his dribble unless he is sure he will be shooting or passing the ball.

If 1 decides to pass the ball to a player cutting to the basket, he'll have to make the pass so that the cutter can catch the ball without having to slow down. The cutter needs to hold his hand out to give the ball handler a target to pass to.

All cutters should sprint up the court. A cutter should not assume that he will not receive the ball—if he does and slows down as a result, that will telegraph the play to the defense.

Defend the Play

When a player takes a shot, his teammates should try to get the offensive rebound. However, at least one guard should stay back beyond the 3-point arc, ready to sprint down the court to help prevent a fast break by the other team in case they grab the defensive rebound. If the other team does grab the defensive rebound, the defender guarding the rebounder should play aggressive on-ball defense to block the outlet pass. Keep in mind that teams that like to run the fast break might have the rebounder dribble the ball up the court.

If two guards are playing back instead of one, the guard on the strong side should defend against the ball handler, and the other guard should sprint to the defensive end to try and prevent an easy basket. All the other defenders should sprint down the court. Defenders should never casually backpedal down the court on defense. Keep in mind that players can never run as fast backward as they can forward. Plus, backpedaling can be dangerous because the player is not looking where he is running.

Generally, the first responders (the fastest defenders) should go to the defensive lane area to protect against an easy basket. When the other defenders have caught up (5-on-5 situation), then the defenders can go out to guard their assigned opponents.

In a 5-on-5 situation, the defender guarding the ball should sprint, rather than slide or side-shuffle, to catch up and get between the ball handler

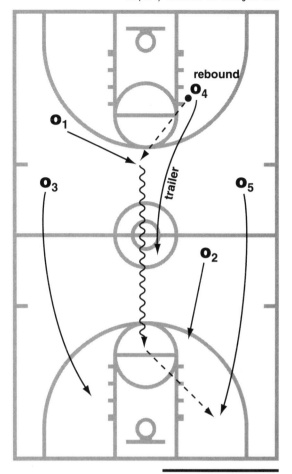

Fast break with rebound and outlet.

and the basket. He should play good on-ball defense, including trying to force the player to dribble to his weaker side. However, if the defense is out-manned on a fast break, the first priority is to defend the basket. In a 2-on-1 fast break this may mean that the defensive player may need to concede a jump shot by the ball handler, but that's usually better than overplaying the ball handler and leaving another player open under the basket for a quick pass and then an easy uncontested layup. If there's help in the form of at least one more defender in the paint (say, in a 3-plus-on-2 fast break—that is, three or more offensive players versus two defensive players), then the defense has the luxury of having one defender challenge the ball handler. But even in this situation, the remaining defender should defend the basket, committing only when a cutter close to the basket has received the ball. Communication among the defenders is key because the defense should try not to leave any opponent open under the basket.

Beating the Press

Run the Play

Player 4 is out-of-bounds with the ball looking to make an inbounds pass to a teammate.

Players 1 and 2 position themselves in a stack, and prepare to break in opposite directions.

Players 3 and 5 stand at half court.

Players 1 and 2 free each other up and break in opposite directions.

Player 4 passes the ball to 1, who dribbles up the court.

Player 5 breaks to the strong side of the court.

Player 1 can continue to dribble or pass the ball to either 3 or 5.

Player 1 can pass the ball to the trailer, 4, if necessary.

The team then runs a fast break or a set play from this book.

Focus on Fundamentals

This play is designed to help move the ball up the court when the defense plays *full-court pressure defense*—aggressive defense to impede the progress of the ball up the court. The offense has 10 seconds to move the ball past half court.

Player 5 breaks to the strong side of the court to give the ball handler two targets to pass to on the strong side, as a pass by the ball handler across the court to the weak side could be intercepted. So if 2 is the ball handler, then 5 would stay, and 3 would move to the strong side (diagram 2).

If the defense tries to trap the ball handler, this means that there is a player who is not being guarded. It's not only up to the ball handler to find the open player, it's imperative that the open player be proactive and get to a place on the floor where the ball handler can pass him the ball.

To avoid traps, the ball handler should try not to dribble near the corners (or the sidelines) because those are good places to back a dribbler into

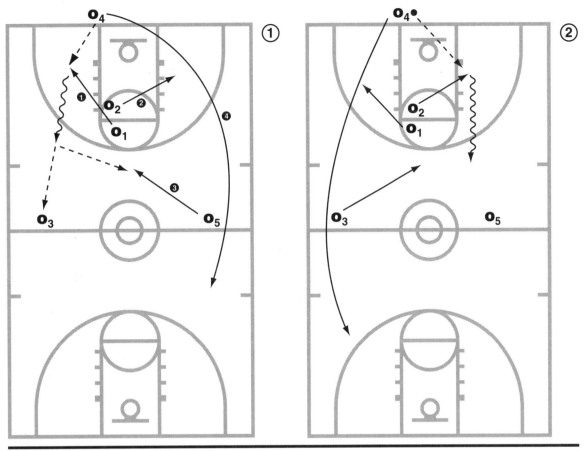

Beating the press. ① Player 4 inbounds to 1. ② With 2 as the ball handler, 3 moves to the strong side.

a corner. Also, the ball handler should not pick up his dribble unless he knows he will be passing or shooting the ball.

Defend the Play

When a player takes a shot, his teammates should try to get the offensive rebound. However, at least one guard should stay back beyond the 3-point arc, ready to sprint down the court to help prevent a fast break by the other team in case they grab the defensive rebound. If the other team does grab the defensive rebound, the defender guarding the rebounder should play aggressive on-ball defense to block the outlet pass. Keep in mind that teams that like to run the fast break might have the rebounder dribble the ball up the court.

If two guards are playing back instead of one, the guard on the strong side should defend against the ball handler, and the other guard should sprint to the defensive end to try and prevent an easy basket. All the other defenders should sprint down the court. Defenders should never casually backpedal down the court on defense. Keep in mind that players can never run as fast backward as they can forward. Plus, backpedaling can be dangerous because the player is not looking where he is running.

Generally, the first responders (the fastest defenders) should go to the defensive lane area to protect against an easy basket. When the other defenders have caught up (5-on-5 situation), then the defenders can go out to guard their assigned opponents.

In a 5-on-5 situation, the defender guarding the ball should sprint, rather than slide or side-shuffle, to catch up and get between the ball handler and the basket. He should play good on-ball defense, including trying to force the player to dribble to his weaker side. However, if the defense is outmanned on a fast break, the first priority is to defend the basket. In a 2-on-1 fast break this may mean that the defensive player may need to concede a jump shot by the ball handler, but that's usually better than overplaying the ball handler and leaving another player open under the basket for a quick pass and then an easy uncontested layup. If there's help in the form of at least one more defender in the paint (say, in a 3-plus-on-2 fast break—that is, three or more offensive players versus two defensive players), then the defense has the luxury of having one defender challenge the ball handler. But even in this situation, the remaining defender should defend the basket, committing only when a cutter close to the basket has received the ball. Communication among the defenders is key because the defense should try not to leave any opponent open under the basket.

CHAPTER 10

Inbounds Plays

This chapter offers basic inbounds plays that cover three scenarios. These include an inbounds play from the sideline to counter aggressive half-court presses, an inbounds play from your opponent's baseline to counter aggressive full-court presses, and an inbounds play from the baseline behind your own basket to get the ball into play in your offensive zone.

Inbounds from Sideline

Run the Play

Player 3 is out-of-bounds with the ball looking to make an inbounds pass to a teammate.

    The other players set up in a box formation.

    Player 2 screens for 1.

    Player 1 uses the screen to cut to the sideline.

    Player 2 rolls in the opposite direction to the sideline.

    Player 3 inbounds a pass to 1 or 2.

Focus on Fundamentals

If the ball goes out-of-bounds over the sidelines, the team will have to make an inbounds pass from the sideline to resume play. Typically, the defense will try to contest the inbounds pass by playing aggressive denial defense. The inbounds passer will have only 5 seconds to get the ball inbounds, standing from the spot designated by the referee. So it's best to designate your best passer as the player to make the inbounds pass.

Defend the Play

Player X3 should play aggressive on-ball defense to obstruct 3's view.

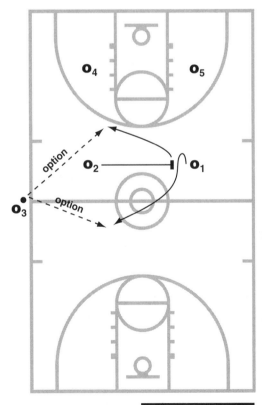

Inbounds from sideline.

Players X1 and X2 should communicate who will cover the screener and who will cover the screen cutter.

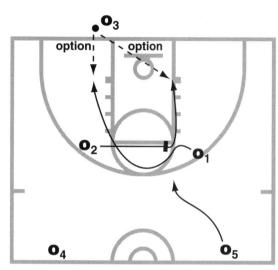

Inbounds from defensive baseline.

Inbounds from Defensive Baseline

Run the Play

Player 3 is out-of-bounds with the ball looking to make an inbounds pass to a teammate.

    The other players set up in a box formation.

    Player 2 screens for 1.

    Player 1 uses the screen to cut to the baseline.

    Player 2 rolls in the opposite direction to the baseline.

    Player 3 inbounds a pass to 1 or 2.

Focus on Fundamentals

If the opposing team scores a basket, then your team gets possession of the ball. Your player takes the ball to the out-of-bounds side of the baseline, and makes an inbounds pass to a teammate who brings the ball up the court. Sometimes the defense allows the ball to be passed inbounds uncontested. Other times (for example, near the end of a close game), the defense plays aggressive denial defense.

    To help improve his inbounds passing angle, the player making the inbounds pass is allowed to run along the out-of-bounds side of the baseline and make the inbounds pass from any point along that line. It's best, however, if he doesn't lob pass the ball from directly underneath the basket because the ball might hit and deflect off the backboard or support structures.

    Whoever receives the inbounds pass has the option to run a fast-break play.

Defend the Play

Players X1 and X2 should communicate who will cover the screener and who will cover the screen cutter.

Inbounds with Diagonal Roll (Frontcourt)

Run the Play

Player 1 is out-of-bounds with the ball looking to make an inbounds pass to a teammate.

    The other players set up in a box formation.

    Player 4 screens for 5.

    Player 5 fakes a cut to the wing, and then uses the screen to cut to the opposite corner.

    Player 4 rolls down the lane toward the basket.

    Meantime, 3 breaks to the corner.

    Player 1 inbounds a pass to 4 or 5.

Focus on Fundamentals

If the opposing team swats the ball out-of-bounds in your offensive zone or commits a nonshooting foul, then your team retains possession of the ball, but must restart play by making an inbounds pass from the baseline behind its own basket or the sideline, whichever is closer.

Spacing. Player 3 needs to clear to the corner to make room for 4 rolling into the lane. Player 2 needs to pop out a bit to make room for 5 cutting to the basket, but at the same time be ready to receive a pass at the wing from 5.

Defend the Play

Players X4 and X5 should communicate who will cover the screener and who will cover the screen cutter.

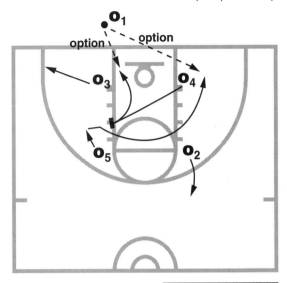

Inbounds with diagonal roll.

Inbounds with Down Screens

Run the Play

Player 1 is out-of-bounds with the ball looking to make an inbounds pass to a teammate.

The other players set up in a box formation.

Players 4 and 5 screen for 2 and 3.

Players 2 and 3 initiate their scissor cuts to the basket.

Players 2 and 3 coordinate their cuts to make X2 and X3 bump into each other.

Players 2 and 3 use the screens to get open along the baseline.

Meantime, 4 and 5 step toward the ball.

Player 1 inbounds a pass to 2, 3, 4, or 5.

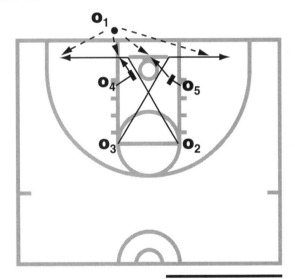

Inbounds with down screens.

Focus on Fundamentals

Spacing. Players 4 and 5 should be careful not to stay in the lane for too long to avoid a 3-second violation.

Defend the Play

All defenders should communicate who will cover the screener and who will cover the screen cutter.

CHAPTER 11

Quick Hitters

A *quick hitter* is a set play used to get the ball quickly to your best player so that she can score. We've only included two because the goal of youth basketball should be to develop all your players, not just the "best" ones. These plays are good for end-of-game or other situations where you need to try and get more points on the board quickly and efficiently.

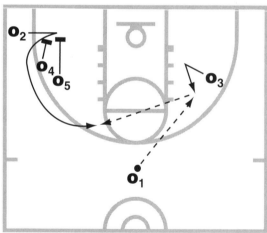

Catch and shoot off double screen.

Catch and Shoot off Double Screen

Run the Play

Player 1 passes the ball to 3.

Players 4 and 5 double screen for 2. A *double screen* is when two offensive players set screens on a single defender, with the goal of confusing the defenders—the three defenders have to decide whether to switch and who should switch.

Player 2 uses the screen to cut to the wing.

Scoring opportunity. Player 3 passes the ball to 2 for the jump shot.

Focus on Fundamentals

The screen cutter should be your team's best long-range shooter.

Defend the Play

Players X3, X4, and X5 should communicate who will cover the screeners and who will cover the screen cutter.

Catch and Shoot off Down Screen (1-2-2 Set)

Run the Play

Player 5 down screens for 3.

Player 3 uses the screen to pop out to the top of the key.

Scoring opportunity. Player 1 passes the ball to 3 for the jump shot.

Focus on Fundamentals

The screen cutter should be your team's best long-range shooter.

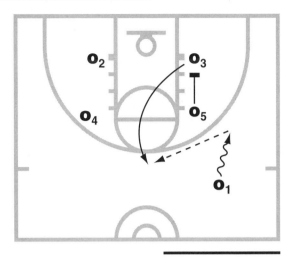

Catch and shoot off down screen.

Defend the Play

Players X3 and X5 should communicate who will cover the screener and who will cover the screen cutter.

Second Options

Scoring opportunity. If 3 can't get open, 1 is in a good position at the wing to pass the ball to 5 in the low post. Player 5 can then make a power move basket.

The Fundamentals

Part One, The Playbook, is this book's main order of business. Other books cover fundamental basketball skills in greater detail than we have room to do in Part Two. We recommend *The Baffled Parent's Guide to Coaching Youth Basketball, The Baffled Parent's Guide to Coaching Girls' Basketball,* and *The Baffled Parent's Guide to Great Basketball Drills.*

Still, you need an immediate context for coaching the offensive plays in Part One, and we aim to provide that in the following sections. Familiarity with the terminology and concepts discussed in Part Two is essential to a good understanding of how the plays work and how to defend against them.

Note that we've used **bold** to emphasize the featured skills and concepts.

Basic Defense

Nothing is more central to coaching and playing offense than understanding how defense is played. Good defense can disrupt a play or even prevent one from beginning in the first place. Let's say, for example, that the offense wants to run a play requiring a pass from the wing into the low post. If the defense is able to prevent the entry pass from the point guard to the wing from taking place, then the offense will have to adjust by making V-cuts or other moves to get open, or even perhaps by using another play from its playbook. Some offenses will be able to adjust quickly, but many at the youth level will not be able to adjust and will become frustrated and turn the ball over.

Spacing Sense

Keep in mind that your players need to understand the key role that **spacing** plays in good man-to-man defense. Start with the concepts of ball side (or strong side) versus help side (or weak side). Picture the court as being split into two halves by an imaginary line running from one basket to the other. The side of the court the ball is on is the **ball side**, and the other side is the **weak side**. Another factor is whether the offensive player being guarded is closer to the basket than the ball is. If he is, and if he's on the ball side of the court, that's a cue for the defender to deny him the ball. Otherwise, the defender will need to adjust so he can help out his teammates.

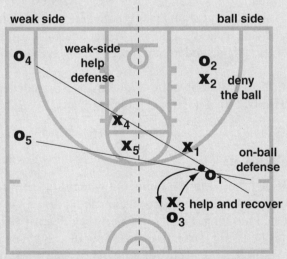

Apply **on-ball defense** when guarding the player with the ball. **Deny the ball** when guarding a player without the ball who is on the ball side of the court and closer to the basket than the ball is. If the ball is closer to the basket than the player being guarded, the defender should **help and recover**. Weak-side defenders help out by getting into **weak-side help defense** position. Each of these tactics is discussed in more detail in the text.

The foregoing merely underscores what you already know: Teaching good defense not only helps your players respond to it on offense but also helps them stay in games when their offense isn't working. Even if your team is missing many of its shots or turning the ball over on offense, it can give itself a fighting chance by playing relentless defense.

Most youth teams have a wide range of player talent and size. Not every player is going to be a great shooter or playmaker right away, but playing smart hustle defense is a way for every player on the team (big and small) to make an immediate high-impact contribution. Teaching and preaching good defense will help keep every player on the team (including potential late bloomers) interested in the game until their other skills start to improve.

It's critical for young players to learn the core skill of playing man-to-man defense, including how to quickly and seamlessly move from on-ball to off-ball defense and back again, depending on where the offensive players are relative to the ball and the basket. Therefore, we do not encourage teaching zone defense (where defenders are assigned areas or "zones" of the court rather than being assigned players to guard) to youth teams. You may be tempted at times to abandon man-to-man for zone defense, especially after your team gets beat up by an opponent who drives consistently into the lane and causes mass confusion among your players. Our best advice is not to give up on man-to-man!

Each play in Part One includes tips on how to defend the play using man-to-man defense. After your players master how to execute a play in this book, consider adding defenders and running the play as a drill, in a gamelike manner.

Let's take a closer look at how good man-to-man defense can help disrupt plays. Think of these tactics as defensive "plays" you can use to counter the offensive plays in this book.

On-Ball Defense

Teams are at their best and most efficient when they can run plays with quick player movements, crisp passing, and little dribbling. When a player dribbles the ball too long, this should alert your defense that the opposing team may still be trying to set up or that nobody can get open to begin a play. At the youth level, lots of dribbling may simply mean indecision on the part of the ball handler or a lack of confidence in his teammates. Lots of dribbling may also mean that the dribbler has not yet mastered the skill of heads-up dribbling (see the discussion on dribbling on pages 97–99). If he's dribbling with his head down and his eyes on the ball, he has no idea what his teammates are doing or even where they are. In these situations, the player defending the dribbler should keep up the defensive pressure rather than let up.

Defending against the triple threat. ① Daniel, the offensive player, is in the **triple threat position**, meaning he can pass, shoot, or dribble. As defender, Jerome's main goal is to try to prevent the ball from getting closer to the basket. He plays **pressure defense**, staying close to the ball (about an arm's length away) and positioning himself on the straight line between the ball and the basket (the **passing line**). He uses his hand to **trace the ball**: too far, and Jerome gives Daniel an open look; too close, and Daniel could drive right by. Jerome also has his left foot forward to try to **force** the right-handed Daniel to dribble to his left side. ② When Daniel starts to dribble, Jerome reacts by quickly sliding his feet to stay between Daniel and the basket. He stays low, taking care not to cross his feet. ③ If Daniel **picks up his dribble**—stops dribbling altogether—Jerome closes in to take away Daniel's space, using his hands to prevent a pass or shot. If Daniel is out of shooting range when he gives up his dribble, consider having the defender **sag off** the ball toward the basket and anticipate the next pass. (Note that sagging off is recommended only for advanced players with good judgment; young players should closely guard a player who has picked up his dribble.)

Defending against the shot. Now Jerome is playing offense and Daniel is defending against him. As Jerome takes the shot, Daniel should not try to block the shot by smacking down on the ball—a surefire way to get whistled for a foul. Rather, Daniel should try to **alter the shot** by blocking Jerome's vision. If he can block the shot with up-stretched fingers, so much the better. After Jerome shoots the ball, Daniel should promptly **block out** to prevent Jerome from getting a rebound of his own shot. Remind your players to be wary of **pump fakes**, which shooters use to get defenders to overcommit. For example, a defender can **overcommit** by prematurely jumping into the air to defend what he thinks will be a shot. As soon as the defender takes to the air, the offensive player drives to the basket. A defender should try not to leave his feet until the shooter does.

Explain to the team that the purpose of aggressive defense is to cause **turnovers** and **disrupt plays**. Defenders who **pressure the ball** are not being bullies; they're just playing good defense. In fact, your local league may have a rule that allows the referee to call a violation and award the defense possession of the ball if the defender is able to make the dribbler bounce the ball for longer than 5 seconds without advancing toward the basket. This is the **closely guarded rule**, and it also applies if the defender is able to make his opponent stop dribbling and hold the ball for more than 5 seconds in a row. (Note: It is not a violation to hold the ball 4 seconds, dribble 4 seconds, and hold it another 4 seconds before passing or shooting.)

A lot of youth players tend to think of defense as being strictly reactive, when the best defenders play defense proactively. When pressuring the ball, players should try to position themselves to force the dribbler to dribble with his weak hand. Unless the dribbler is confident with both hands, he'll probably get nervous, giving the defense yet another opportunity to disrupt the play.

Deny the Ball

Defensive players must work together if they are to have any chance of disrupting a play in progress or to prevent one from starting. While the

Denying the ball. ① Coach Dunphy tries to pass the ball to Jihad (far left) on the wing. Matt denies the ball by getting into a good defensive stance, with one hand (his **denial hand**) and one foot in the **passing line** (the straight line between the ball and the receiver), while keeping an eye on the ball and Jihad at the same time. ② Jihad is starting to make a backdoor cut. In response Matt changes direction by turning his head and switching his denial hand.

Denying the low post. ① Jihad (right) is denying Matt the ball in the low post by getting in the **three-quarters position**, with his front foot and hand more or less in the **passing line**, while keeping an eye on the ball. **Post players** seek contact in order to control and seal out defenders. The defender can use his lower body to try to prevent the offensive player from getting even closer to the basket. ② Jihad defends the post by **fronting** (guarding a player by standing directly in front of him) Matt, but this may give Matt the rebounding advantage, since Jihad won't be able to block out Matt. If the defense fronts, the offensive post player should **walk up the line**—force the defender farther from the basket. This will give the post player plenty of room to change direction and go toward the basket to receive an overhead lob pass.

The defensive players (X2 and X3) on the ball side of the court deny the ball by getting between the ball and any potential receiver in scoring position (O2 and O3). Note that O2 and O3 are closer to the basket than the ball is.

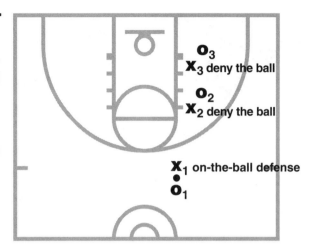

defender guarding the ball is applying **on-ball defense** to prevent a shot or a pass from leaving the ball handler's hands, the other defenders have to try to **deny the pass**—stop the other players who are in scoring position on the ball side of the court from receiving a pass. An offensive player without the ball on the ball side of the court is in scoring position if he is closer to the basket than the ball is.

Help and Recover

For any number of reasons, including good spacing, not all the offensive players on the floor will be in scoring position at the same time during a

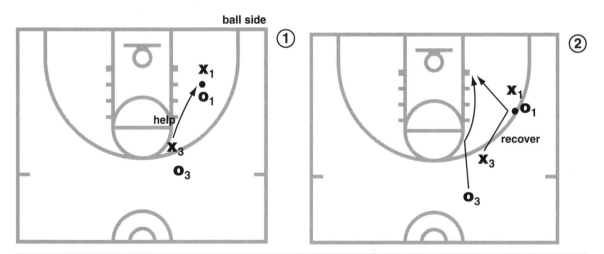

Help and recover. ① Player O3 is not a scoring threat because he is farther away from the basket than the ball is. So X3 doesn't need to deny O3 the ball even though O3 is on the ball side of the court. Instead, X3 goes to **help** X1 **pressure the ball**. If X3 is able to get close enough, X3 can help X1 **trap** the ball handler (without fouling him) and make him stop dribbling, inducing a violation if the ball handler can't get rid of the ball in 5 seconds. ② If X1 is able to contain the ball handler all by himself, then X3 **recovers** by finding O3 and guarding him. If O1 dribbles or passes the ball to the weak side, then X3 has to adjust and get into his **weak-side help defense** position.

play. Rather, one or more of the players may be farther from the basket than the ball is. In this case, the defender may have to temporarily abandon his man, help his teammate pressure the ball to prevent the ball from going toward the basket, and then recover by going back to guard his man.

Penetration Defense

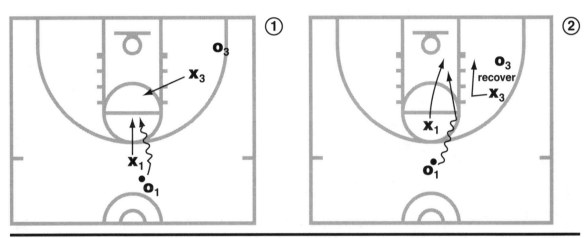

Penetration defense. ① Player X3 is playing **denial defense** against O3. Player O1 beats X1 and starts to drive to the basket. Player X3 goes to **help**. ② Players X3 and X1 must communicate to decide whether they will **switch** or whether X1 will be able to sprint fast enough to **recover** against O1, enabling X3 to recover against O3.

Weak-Side Help Defense

A defensive player guarding an offensive player on the weak side of the floor needs to pay attention to both the player he is guarding and the ball. He should be about midway between his assigned player and the ball and slightly off the passing line to be in a good position to prevent the ball handler from driving into the lane or a lobbing a pass across the court to the weak side. Defenders always need to reposition as the ball moves. If the weak-side player gets closer to the ball, then the weak-side defender needs to move from midway to closer to the weak-side player he is guarding. If your weak-side players consistently put themselves in a position to help out, then your team may force your opponents to think twice before driving to the hole or using plays that call for passing to players that cut into the lane.

Weak-side help defense. ① Each defensive player on the **weak side** (such as Juan, far left) should position himself so that he is about midway between the ball handler (Nafis, far right) and the weak-side player he is guarding (Peyton, middle). Juan is not directly on the **passing line**, but rather positions himself slightly off the line so that he can see both the ball and the weak-side player he is guarding. Notice that Juan is the "peak" of a shallow triangle between the ball and his opponent. He gets into a good **defensive stance** with one arm extended toward the ball, and the other toward Peyton, the weak-side player he is guarding, making sure to keep an eye on both. Some coaches like to call this an **open stance**. ② Juan is in a good position to be able to help defend against the ball handler (Nafis) who has beaten his man (Kevin) and is driving toward the basket. If Juan started by guarding his man too closely, instead of playing **weak-side help defense**, he would leave an open pathway to the basket for the ball handler to drive straight through.

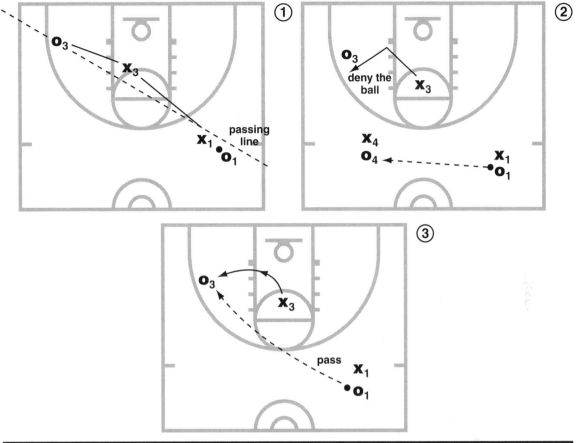

Weak-side help defense. ① Player X3 has positioned himself about midway between O3 and the ball. Note how X3 is already in a good position to **help** out if O1 beats X1 and drives to the basket. ② If O1 dribbles the ball to the side of the court X3 is on (or passes the ball to O4), then that side becomes the strong side, and X3 quickly will have to switch to **denial** or **help-and-recover mode**, depending on whether O3 is farther or closer to the basket than the ball is. ③ If O1 manages to pass the ball to O3, then X3 has to quickly move from **help mode** to **on-ball defense**. Rather than run straight at O3, X3 cuts to the basket and then approaches O3 from the direction of the basket. Taking this angle helps prevent O3 from driving straight to the basket.

Defending Screens
We'll discuss how to defend screens in the Screening section, which begins on page 116.

Traps

Traps. ① The ball handler (Jerome) has dribbled himself into a corner. The defenders (Jihad and Daniel) avoid contact, but move their feet to block all possible escape routes for the ball handler. The defenders move their hands and arms to prevent the offensive player from passing the ball. Note how the defenders use the sideline and baseline as an extra defender. ② The offensive player (Coach Dunphy) looks for escape routes. For example, here the defenders leave a wide enough opening for Coach Dunphy to step and dribble through the gap without drawing an offensive foul. Remind your players that if they are being trapped by two or more players, that means that there is at least one completely open teammate on the floor.

Individual Offensive Moves

The previous section covered the defensive context for running the plays in Part One. Now we establish the offensive context for the Part One plays, which is all about the way each player executes the chosen play. It should be clear by now that no play succeeds by virtue of its conceptual brilliance. Success depends on execution.

Think of each play in this book as a choreographed sequence of **individual offensive moves** or **plays within plays**. In a hard-fought game, the defensive players will **pressure**, **deny**, **help out**, and try to **disrupt a play** by preventing passes or blocking shots. Sometimes the offense will have no choice but to abandon one play and try to run another, but most of the time the offense relies on individual moves to adjust to the defense and allow the chosen play to continue. For example, if a play calls for the player in the low post to receive a pass and shoot the ball, he doesn't just give up and kick the ball back out as soon as the defender puts up his hands. Rather the low post player adjusts by making a fake or other move to create the space he needs to shoot. Remind your players that they're not being ball hogs when they use individual offensive moves—as long as they use the moves to help the team run its plays.

Basic Dribble

Remind your team that every player, not just the point guard, is a playmaker and should learn the fundamentals of good dribbling—which means fingertip dribbling with the head up and, when guarded, adopting an athletic stance while protecting the ball with the other hand and the body. It's important to reinforce the concept that each player needs to **see the floor** at all times, even while dribbling the ball. He'll need to see how his teammates and defenders are positioned so that the team can take advantage of defensive mismatches and errors, find the open man, and capitalize on scoring opportunities. While heads-up playmaking requires the kind of awareness that takes years to develop, it begins with the basics, such as mastering good dribbling skills.

Basic dribble. Taylor keeps her head up to **see the court** while dribbling and uses only her fingertips, not her palm. A good dribbler should be adept at dribbling with either hand and should be able to change direction or pace (walk, run, or hesitate) while dribbling.

A good dribbler is not an idle dribbler. He dribbles with a purpose, actively looking to move the ball to a better position on the court so that he can initiate or continue a play in progress. The plays in this book are diagrammed as if run in a vacuum, but during a game, the defense will do everything it can to **disrupt a play**, including **pressuring the ball** and **denying passes**. So while the intended receiver is making his V-cut or other move to get open, the ball handler may need to dribble a few steps to improve the **passing angle** or to elude his defender. A good dribbler will not stand in one spot dribbling (or worse, give up his dribble) and wait for his teammates to get open—that will invite the defense to close ranks and overplay. When it's time to stop dribbling, he should aim for a two-foot **jump stop** (come to a complete stop, legs apart and knees bent). Then he can use either foot as the **pivot foot**, which will give him more movement options. Many players, however, find it easier to shoot a quick jump shot off the dribble if they stop while the trail foot is still in the air.

On the other hand, remind your players not to dribble (or pass) into crowded areas of the court or into corners, and to watch for **traps**. Defenders like to double-team and trap in the corners and sometimes at midcourt along the sidelines. Good spacing is important, and a player who dribbles into traffic risks turning the ball over.

Crossover dribble. ① Nafis is able to quickly change direction with his crossover dribble. ② He dribbles with his fingertips and with his head up, surveying the floor for any offensive opportunities.

Crossover Dribble

In a **crossover dribble** the player makes a quick, hard dribble in front of and across his body to the other hand. The ball should bounce in front of his feet and stay below his knees so the defender can't steal or deflect it during the crossover. This move is used to quickly change direction, to fake the

defender, to protect the ball from the defender's reach, or to create a better passing angle.

Drive to the Basket

Many of the plays in Part One seek to create scoring opportunities by passing the ball to a player who is cutting to the basket. Just as often, however, an opportunity to drive to the basket arises unexpectedly in the middle of executing a set play or a continuity offense. Whenever a player with the ball finds himself in a good position to **drive to the basket**, score a **layup**, and perhaps draw a **foul**, he should take it. Players should never drive directly into traffic, but they should always be on the lookout for defensive breakdowns and openings. For example, if the player with the ball sees that all the defenders are overplaying and in poor position to help out, leaving the lane wide open, this may be a good opportunity to **take it to the hole** (drive to the basket). If defensive help arrives, the driver can **kick it out** (pass it to an open player for a jump shot).

Drive to the basket. Juan (right) is guarding Kevin in a staggered stance, with his left foot slightly forward in order to force the right-handed ball handler to the left. Kevin responds by attempting to drive to his right because he wants to attack Juan's front foot. If Kevin can get past Juan's front foot, he'll have the advantage because Juan will need to pivot before attempting to catch up.

INDIVIDUAL OFFENSIVE MOVES

Fake-Out Moves, Basic to Intermediate *(see text, page 104)*

Low post fake followed by a pivot for a jump hook. ① The offensive player (Matt) receives the ball in the low post, where he has established position just outside the lane to avoid a 3-second violation. His back is to the basket, and his **stance** is wide to **seal off** the defender. His right foot is his pivot foot. He fakes toward the baseline with his head, his upper body, and the ball. ②, ③ When the defender (Jenn) moves in the direction of the fake, Matt **pivots** the other way, takes a quick dribble into the lane, and takes a **jump hook shot**.

Jab step and same-side drive. ① From a **triple threat position**, the offensive player (Daniel) fakes by leaning forward while taking a short **jab step** with his right foot, which is his nonpivot foot. ②, ③ If his defender (Peyton) does not respond, then Daniel lifts the same foot to take a longer step past the defender and explode with a dribble to the basket. Some coaches call this a **hesitation move** because the offensive player pauses slightly after the jab step while gauging the defender's reaction.

Rocker step: jab step, recoil, and same-side drive. ① From a **triple threat position**, the offensive player (Daniel) fakes by leaning forward while taking a short **jab step** with his nonpivot foot, in this case, his right foot. ② If his defender (Peyton) reacts to the jab step by retreating, Daniel can **recoil** (pull back the jab foot) and use the newly created space for a better passing angle or to take a jump shot. ③ If the defender steps back in toward the offensive player or overcommits by getting airborne after the offensive player recoils, the offensive player can use the nonpivot foot to take a long step past the front foot of the defender and explode with a dribble to the basket. This is called a **rocker step**—a play in which the offensive player makes a **jab step** in one direction and then follows it by driving by the defender in that direction.

Jab step and other-side drive. ① From a **triple threat position**, the offensive player (Nafis) fakes by leaning forward while taking a **jab step** with his nonpivot foot. (Note that the jab step with the nonpivot foot, here the right foot, should be shorter than shown.) ②, ③ If his defender (Kevin) reacts by moving in the direction of the step, Nafis can bring the ball and his jab foot across his body, initiate a dribble with the hand on the pivot-foot side, and **drive** the other way, exploding past the defender. From this point he can drive to the basket, let defensive help come to him and pass to the open man, or square up for a jump shot.

Fake and cut to receive the ball. ① Coach Dunphy (at the point) wants to pass the ball to Jerome (far right) at the wing, but Taylor is playing tough **denial defense** to prevent the pass. In response, Jerome cuts toward the basket while watching the passer out of the corner of his eye. ② When Taylor commits to Jerome's initial cut, Jerome plants his inside foot and explosively cuts back toward the wing to receive the ball.

Fakes are used to shake off defenders and create just enough space for an offensive opportunity. The goal is to get the defender's momentum moving in the direction of the fake, then immediately reverse direction to dribble, pass, or take a shot.

The photos show various fake-out moves. Players can practice direct **drives**, **jab steps**, and **pivots**, and then add the **recoil** and the **crossover**

dribble, practicing them in isolation, then in sequence, and later against defenders. To fake, a player moves the ball, perhaps while taking a step with his nonpivot foot, in the direction he wants the defender to move. He can also fake with his head and upper body. He should keep the ball close to his body so he can protect it. A fake should be done at medium speed in order to make the defender move. Once the defender moves in that direction, the player quickly reverses direction—whether it's to explode for a drive to the basket, make a quick jump shot, or pass the ball. **Medium speed** means moving with conviction, but not so quickly that the defender has no time to take the bait. A fake that's over before the player can react is ineffective.

In some situations the offensive player will want to lull his defender into thinking that there's nothing going on. In such a case the player may need to walk or drift before exploding in his intended direction.

There are many ways to combine fakes, pivots, and other footwork to throw off defenders. As your players develop, they'll eventually learn what fakes and combinations work best in different situations, as well as learn new skills like how to fake while dribbling using an assortment of spin moves and half-spin moves. They'll also learn to think on their feet and improvise as advanced defenders learn how to counter their fakes. But keep in mind that even the fanciest footwork is a combination of basic fundamental moves.

Pivot Moves

The **pivot** is an important maneuver used in many plays. A player who grabs a defensive rebound is likely to be facing the basket, and will need to land and then pivot away from the player guarding him to make an **outlet pass**. A player who catches the ball coming from one direction during a set play may need to pivot to make a pass in another direction. A low post player will need to be able to catch the ball and pivot in either direction for a quick **power move basket**. Players need to master pivoting, because once a player catches a ball, he can't move both feet unless he jumps to make a pass or shot. Otherwise, lifting or dragging the pivot foot is a violation.

Jump stop. Matt catches the ball as both feet hit the floor at the same time so he can use either foot as the pivot foot. This is a **two-foot jump stop**. Sometimes a player catches the ball as one foot hits the floor, and then the other follows. This is **one-two stop**. The first foot to land becomes his **pivot foot**, and it has to stay on the floor unless he decides to pass or shoot. He can change the direction he's facing by pivoting his body on this foot, but he has to stay low or he'll lose his balance.

Popout Moves

A **popout** describes the movement that an offensive player who is closer to the basket makes when a play calls for him to go to the **pivot**, **high post**, or **wing** areas to set a screen or receive a pass.

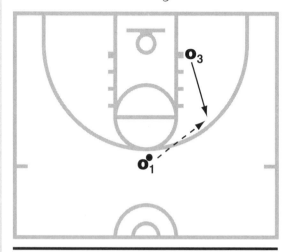

Basic popout. Player O3 **pops out** from the block to receive the entry pass from O1 to start the play.

Advanced popout. Player O3 walks to where X3 can no longer see both O3 and the ball, and then **pops out** (sprints to the top of the key) to receive the pass in the high post.

Post-Up Moves

Low-to-medium post, defender behind. ① Juan (left) is playing **denial defense** in the **three-quarters position** against Jihad in the low post. Jihad **posts up** on the block and should use his hips (not his arms or hands) and a wide stance to push back and **seal out** and keep Juan behind him in order to create a bigger passing area. ② Jihad **squares up** to the path of the pass and has his hands up to give the passer a target. An advanced post player will try to catch the ball with both feet in the air, and make a **jump stop** so he can use either foot as his pivot foot. ③, ④ Jihad receives the pass with his elbows out and the ball under the chin to protect it, **pivots** (drop-steps to get toward the basket in front of Juan), takes one dribble, and makes a **power move shot** against the glass. Jihad should then block out and go for the rebound. If other defenders converge to help out, he can kick it back out to the open man for a jump shot.

Posting up describes how an offensive player—the **post player**—who is usually within close range of the basket and often, but not always, with his back to the basket, uses his hips and quick feet to **seal out** the **post defender**; that is, he pushes the defender into a position where the defender cannot effectively **deny the pass**. The post player can then receive a pass, and use various **pivots** and **fake-out moves** to make an inside shot. Any player, big or small, can become a good post-up player if he uses good technique and is not afraid of contact. A player becomes a post player anytime he plays in the low-to-medium post area with his back to the basket against a similarly sized or smaller player.

Low-to-medium post, defender fronting. ① The defender, Juan (left), is **fronting** Jihad, the post player, in the low post. Jihad should use his hips (not his arms or hands) and a wide stance to **walk the defender up the line**—push Juan forward (away from the basket) toward the passer to create a bigger passing area for a possible lob pass behind the post player. ② Coach Dunphy shows Jihad how to position himself for an overhead lob pass. Once Jihad receives the pass, he will be able to make a **power move shot** against the glass.

Squaring up. Coach Dunphy teaches Jenn the concept of **squaring up** to the basket.

Square-Up Moves

Squaring up describes the proper position of the trunk of the player's body when attempting most shots and passes. The horizontal plane of the front trunk of the body should be square to the straight line from the player to his target (the basket or another player). Keep in mind that even a turn-around jump shot (which in most cases is poor shot selection across all skill levels) is released when the front trunk of the body is square to the basket, even though the shooter starts with his back to the basket (is not square).

Triple Threat Position

Triple threat position. Peyton has one hand on top and one hand on the side of the ball. His knees are flexed and he is on the balls of his feet, looking for offensive opportunities. He is in a **triple threat position**, ready to shoot, pass, or dribble.

V-Cut

A player on the wing can use a **V-cut** to get open to receive a pass. To execute a V-cut, the player steps toward his defender (to either side is OK). This may cause a defender who is denying the ball to retreat slightly, giving the player an opening to cut toward the ball to receive the pass. If the defender tries to anticipate the second cut toward the ball, and goes toward the ball instead of retreating, perhaps with the intent of intercepting the pass, the player who started the V-cut can keep going toward the basket and receive a pass for a **backdoor play**. Players on the weak side can also use a V-cut to keep defenders busy while the play is taking place on the other side of the court.

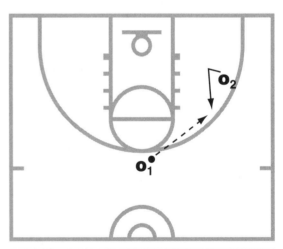

V-cut. Player O2 **V-cuts** to get open to receive the entry pass from O1 to start the play.

Passing

Any kind of pass has the best chance of succeeding if the passer passes the ball while maintaining momentum toward the target. This means that the passer should step toward the target, extend her arms, snap her wrists, and follow through. As your players move into high school, they'll have to learn how to make passes without looking directly at the target while communicating with each other about where the target is cutting and where the pass should be thrown, and still be aware of where the defenders are. If a player looks directly at the target while making a pass, this will telegraph the pass, and the defender may pick it off. Catching the ball is not a passive act, either. The receiver should **jump to the ball** before the defender can get to it.

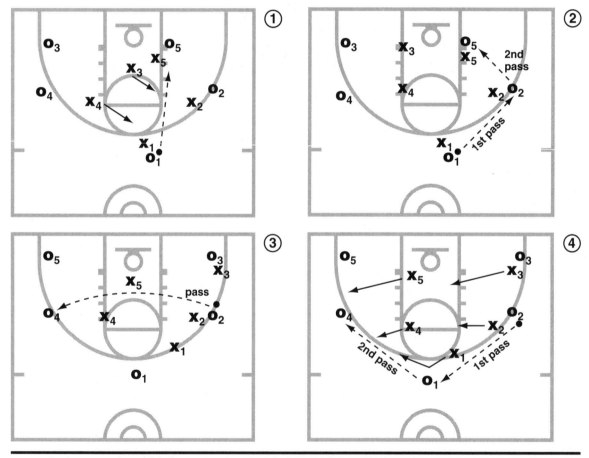

Passing. ① Player O1 at the top of the key attempts a pass into the low post. This is a difficult pass because defenders X3, X4, and X5 are in good position to intercept the pass. ② Player O1 has a better passing angle into the low post by first passing to O2 on the wing, who then passes to O5. ③ If O2 attempts a pass to the weak side, the defensive help players (X4 and X5) are in great position to steal the ball and get a head start for an uncontested layup at the other end of the floor (a **fast break**). ④ If O2 needs to pass the ball to O4 on the weak side, she should first pass it to a player at the top of the key, O1. Spacing is important, too. A player should allow her teammates to balance out the floor, rather than force a pass into a congested area of the court.

She should catch the pass about chest high using soft hands to bring the ball into her body with two hands without bobbling it, land on two feet with a **jump stop**, and get immediately into a **triple threat position**, ready to shoot, drive, or pass, using either foot as her pivot foot.

It's essential that you instill in your players the importance of good passing and catching skills. From a playmaking perspective, good passing requires the passer to be able to see not only where the intended receiver is, but also the location and movements of any defenders who are in a position to intercept the ball. Good passing also requires knowledge of **passing angles**.

A **chest pass** is a standard pass made with two hands from the chest. Younger players may need to start with a **one-handed push pass**, with one hand behind push-passing the ball, the other hand guiding the ball, and with both arms fully extending in the follow-through. Except when throwing a pass all the way down the court, young players should avoid passing with only one hand (without the other hand guiding the ball), especially while dribbling, because it's hard to control one-handed passes. If the passer needs to change his mind, it's almost impossible to stop a one-handed pass once the player starts his motion.

A **bounce pass** is a two-handed pass like a **chest pass**, but it bounces once on the way to its target. The best bounce passes bounce slightly more than halfway to the target so that they arrive between waist and chest level. Bounce passes are best used in situations where the defenders are more or less upright with their hands up, like a pass to the low post or to a player cutting into the lane in traffic. Young players can do a **one-handed push-bounce pass**, with one hand behind push-passing the ball, the other hand guiding the ball, and with both arms fully extending in the follow-through.

An **entry pass** is the first pass that begins a play. In youth play, it is usually but not always made by O1 (the point guard).

An **inbounds pass** is any pass that is made from out-of-bounds onto the court to resume play.

A **lob pass** is any pass made over a defender's head. They are most useful when the defender covering the target is low or when throwing a pass to a tall player playing post-up basketball.

Lob pass. Matt makes a **lob pass** to Jerome in the low post, with Daniel defending (fronting).

Outlet pass. Jihad makes an **outlet pass** with Matt defending.

An **outlet pass** is a pass made by a player on the defensive end of the court, usually promptly after grabbing a defensive rebound and pivoting away from any defenders, to a ball handler to bring the ball up the court.

An **overhead pass** is a pass made starting with two hands over the passer's head. Remind your players to use wrist action to flip the pass. It is often used as an **outlet pass** if delivered with more arm strength.

Rebounding

In executing a play, the offense can do everything right, and yet the shot may still bounce off the rim. On the defensive side, making the offense miss a shot is great, but only if the defense is able to immediately obtain possession of the ball. **Rebounding**—regaining control of the ball after a missed shot— is a critical skill that will enable both sides to run and defend the plays in this book with confidence. **Blocking out** (or **boxing out**) an opposing player after a missed shot will increase a player's chances of grabbing a **rebound**.

Field Goals

The most efficient centers in the NBA usually make less than 60% of their field goal attempts (FGA). The best shooting guards, who play farther from the basket, will usually make less than 45% to 50% of their FGA. If you factor in the "average" players, this means that even players who play basketball for a living miss more than half their shots. Good defense, poor shot selection, and just having an "off" night are some of the reasons players miss their shots. Young players are still developing their shot selection and shooting skills, so field goal percentages (FG%) in youth leagues will be even lower. Therefore, at any level of play, good rebounding helps a team be more successful.

Blocking Out

As soon as a shot is taken, each defensive player has to locate an opposing player to block out. This is usually the offensive player he has been assigned to guard. However, if the offensive player takes a shot off a **screen** by executing a play in this book, the defender won't always be able to **block out** his assigned

Blocking out. ① After Coach Trace takes a shot, Jihad (right), the defensive player, should make contact with and get in front of Matt, the offensive player. ② Jihad faces the basket so he can see the ball bounce off the rim or backboard and then try get the rebound. He **blocks out** Matt, keeping in front of him and using his hips to push back Matt, who is also jostling for position, away from the basket.

player. If the defenders of a screen **switch**, the defenders may have to locate and then block out their new assignments or the closest opposing players.

After blocking out, the defender (and the offensive player) times his jump so that he can grab the rebound at the highest point possible. He should be aggressive, and use two hands to grab the rebound, then land and protect the ball by tucking it near his chin with his elbows out. He should then immediately look for the next scoring or playmaking opportunity, depending on whether it's a defensive or offensive rebound.

Defensive Rebound

A **defensive rebound** is a rebound seized by a defensive player after a missed shot by an opposing player. Once in possession of the ball, the defensive team becomes the offensive team, and the rebounder typically

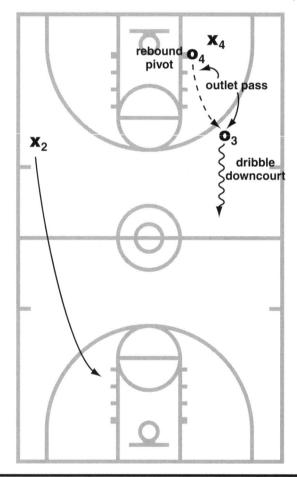

Defensive rebound. At the start of this **fast break**, a defensive player (in this case, O4) grabs a **defensive rebound**, and becomes an offensive player. He **pivots** away from his opponent, and makes the **outlet pass** to a teammate (O3) who shouts "Outlet!" and starts dribbling downcourt. The original shooter, now a defensive player, X2, was the farthest from the basket, so he's the first to sprint down the court to defend against the fast break.

pivots away from any defenders on the ball and then makes an **outlet pass** to a ball handler who **dribbles** the ball past midcourt into the offensive zone. Depending on the situation and how quickly the defense is able to set up, the offensive team can attempt to score using a **fast-break play** or one of the more traditional set plays in this book. Remember never to stifle the creativity of your players, so if a legitimate scoring opportunity occurs suddenly in the middle of a fast-break play, remind your players not to be afraid to improvise.

Offensive Rebound

An **offensive rebound** is a rebound seized by an offensive player after a missed shot by his teammate. Offensive rebounds give the offensive team a fresh start toward another scoring opportunity. When your young players eventually play in advanced leagues that use a shot clock, it will reset to allow the team the full allotted time to attempt another field goal.

If a player grabs an offensive rebound near the basket, there are generally two possible options:

Scoring opportunity. The player should try to avoid putting the ball on the floor after an offensive rebound close to the basket; this only buys time for the defense to react. Rather, he should make a **power move basket** immediately, before the defense has a chance to react, and possibly draw a foul in the process. An advanced athlete very close to the basket might be able to jump into the air and tip or shoot the ball in the basket before landing on his feet.

If it's too congested, and the player is surrounded by opposing players, at least one of his teammates should be open. He should look for an opening, step-dribble through the opening, and pass out to the open player for a quick jump shot or to resume play using another set play from this book.

If a player grabs an offensive rebound farther away from the basket, he'll also have at least two options available:

Scoring opportunity. He should look to drive to the basket (and possibly draw a foul) or take a medium-range jump shot immediately (if he is open and square to the basket) before the defense has a chance to react.

If there's no immediate scoring opportunity, he can look for the open man to resume play using another set play from this book.

Offensive rebound. Matt shoots the ball from close range immediately after grabbing the **offensive rebound**. He jumps as high as he can and shoots a shot off the glass at the peak of his vertical jump.

Screening

Screens (or **picks**) are among the most powerful tools in basketball for creating space and scoring opportunities.

Screening. ① Matt is using a **screen** set by Jihad to get open. Jihad is the **screener** and Matt is the **screen cutter**. The screener gets into a stationary athletic stance close to the defender (not shown) to prevent the defender from guarding the screen cutter. Timing is critical; the screen cutter waits for the screen to be established, and then cuts shoulder to shoulder with the screener after using a **jab step** that draws the defender into the screener. ② Using Jihad's screen Matt successfully breaks free to receive a pass. The same basic shoulder-to-shoulder and timing techniques apply to situations where the screen cutter is dribbling the ball.

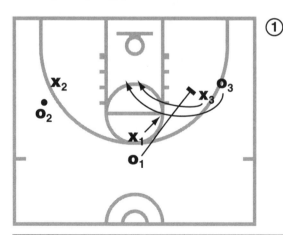
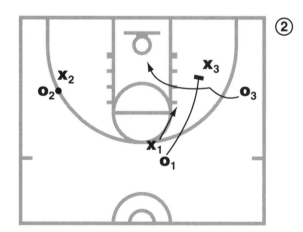

Screening. ① Player O1 sets a screen for O3. But O3 doesn't use the screen effectively and just loops around the screen, giving X3 and X1 plenty of room to follow him through the screen. ② Player O3 effectively uses the screen set for him by cutting shoulder to shoulder with the screener, O1. The defenders have to work together in order to defend screens, and communication is essential. If the defensive players see a screen coming, they should yell "Screen!" If possible, the defender guarding the screen cutter (in this case, X3) should take a series of short steps to **fight over the screen** by sticking out his hips and torso and then stepping over the wide-leg stance of the screener (in this case, O1).

Open slide-through. The defender (Daniel, far left) guarding the **screener** (Jihad, no. 11) steps back slightly to allow the defender (Jerome, second from left) to **slide through** and resume his defense of the **screen cutter** (Matt, no. 10). Daniel needs to recover so he can cover Jihad.

Switch. ①, ② The defender (Daniel, far right) guarding the **screen cutter** (Jihad) gets caught up in the screen set by the **screener** (Matt, no. 10). ③ The defenders switch, and Jerome (far left) jump outs to cover Jihad, the screen cutter. Daniel, who was covering Jihad, switches to cover Matt.

The photos on page 117 show two other ways to defend a screen, the open slide-through and the switch.

Many of the plays in this book employ at least one of the screens described below. Study the diagrams to see how the **screener** works with a **screen cutter** to free up either player.

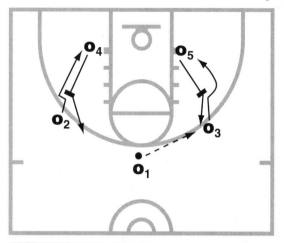

Back screen. Players O4 and O5 **back screen** for O2 and O3. Any of these players has a good chance to free him- or herself from his or her defenders for a pass from O1.

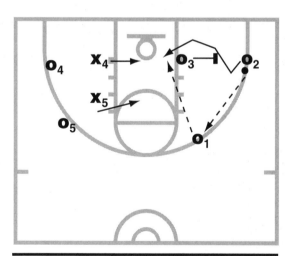

Baseline screen. Player O3 sets a **baseline screen** for O2. Player O2 V-cuts and gets open for a pass from O1. If the defense is doing its job, **weak-side help** defenders (in this case, X4 and X5) will be in or near the lane to protect the basket, and possibly prevent the pass from O1. If the screen is being made in the lane, the screener has to clear the lane quickly before incurring a 3-second violation.

Back Screen

A **back screen** is an offensive play in which a player comes from the low post to set a screen for a player on the perimeter.

Baseline Screen (or Cross Screen)

In this book, a **baseline screen** is any screen in which the screener (whether he's coming from the opposite block or elsewhere) sets a screen near the baseline that the screen cutter uses to cut across the lane.

Down Screen

A **down screen** is a play in which a player comes down from the perimeter to screen for a player in the low post area.

Double Screen

A **double screen** is when two offensive players set screens on a single defender, with the goal of confusing the defenders—the three defenders have to decide whether to switch and who should do it.

Screen Away

A **screen away** is a basic play using a screen to free up a player away from the ball. This book has a number of variations on the screen away.

Two-Screen Sequence

This is a more advanced play. The first screen is used as a kind of decoy for the second screen.

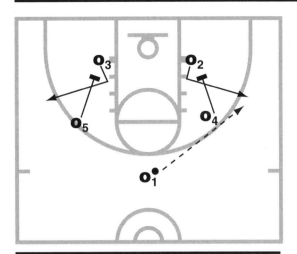

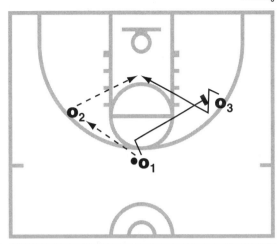

Down screen. Players O4 and O5 **down screen** for O2 and O3. Players O2 and O3 V-cut and use the screens to get open for a pass from O1. If the defense gets confused, both defenders may stay with the screener or with the screen cutter, which may leave either the screener or the screen cutter open for an uncontested shot.

Screen away. Player O1 passes the ball to O2. He then sets a screen for O3 so he can get free for a pass from O2—the **screen away**.

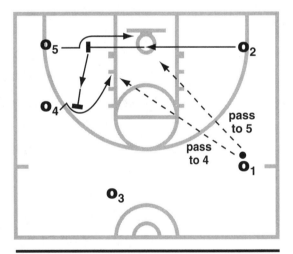

Pass and screen away. Nafis (middle) sets a screen against Coach Langel (right), who is covering Matt (left). Once Nafis sets the screen, Matt cuts close to prevent Coach Langel from fighting over the screen.

Two-screen sequence. Player O2 **baseline screens** for O5, who cuts across the baseline. After setting his screen, O2 **pops out** to set another screen for O4, who cuts to the basket. Player O1 passes the ball to O4 for the layup.

Shooting

Jump Shot

A **jump shot** is any shot taken from a medium to long distance after the
shooter jumps in the air. The youngest players usually shoot from the hip,
and typically shoot as they jump. As they progress, they shoot above the
head at the peak of their vertical leap.

Layup

A **layup** is a shot made from close range as the player drives to the basket.
The best layups are banked in against the backboard.

Jump shots. ①, ②, ③. Matt, Kevin, and Juan demonstrate good **jump shots**.

Layups. ①, ②. Juan and Matt demonstrate good **layups**.

Power Layup

A **power layup** is a two-footed layup.

Sometimes a player driving to the basket finds a defender down low blocking his path. Since the player can't shoot a layup without his forward momentum risking an offensive foul, he makes a sudden **two-foot jump stop**, jumps as high as he can, and shoots the ball off the glass. If the defender is moving, then some players like to lean into the defender to draw the foul. If the defender is already stationary, the player should make the power move and jump straight up to avoid the offensive foul.

A **jump hook** is a quick, explosive shot in which the player's shooting arm goes nearly straight up. This differs from a **hook shot**, where the shooter loops his arm around, which gives the defense an opportunity to strip the ball.

Power layup. Coach Trace instructs Jerome on making a **power layup**.

Power layups. ①, ②, ③.
Jerome demonstrates a good
power layup.

Low post jump hook power move. ① Matt in the low post has his back to the basket. ② He pivots 90 degrees, takes a quick dribble, and then shoots a **jump hook** off the glass. Note that he uses the backboard so he can use the nonshooting side of his body as a buffer against the defender (Jenn).

Glossary

Advance step: A step in which the defender's lead foot steps toward her man, and her back foot slides forward.

Air ball: A shot that hits only air—it misses the rim and the backboard.

Air pass: A pass that goes straight through the air to the receiver.

And one: The *free throw* awarded to a shooter who is fouled as she scores.

Assist: A pass thrown to a player who immediately scores.

Backcourt: The half of the court a team is defending. The opposite of the *frontcourt*. Also refers to a team's guards.

Back cut: A play in which a player plants her outside foot and cuts sharply to the basket.

Backdoor cut: An offensive play in which a player on the perimeter steps away from the basket, drawing the defender with him, and suddenly cuts to the basket behind the defender for a pass. The opposite of a *V-cut*.

Back screen: An offensive play in which a player comes from the *low post* to set a *screen* for a player on the perimeter.

Ball fake: A sudden movement by the player with the ball intended to cause the defender to move in one direction, allowing the passer to pass in another direction. Also called a "pass fake."

Ball reversal: Passing the ball from one side of the court to the other.

Ball screen: An offensive play in which a player sets a *screen* on the defender guarding the player with the ball.

Ball side: The half of the court (if the court is divided lengthwise) that the ball is on. Also called the "strong side." The opposite of the *help side*.

Bank shot: A shot that hits the backboard before hitting the rim or going through the net.

Baseball pass: A one-handed pass thrown like a baseball.

Baseline: The line that marks the playing boundary at each end of the court. Also called the *end line*.

Baseline out-of-bounds play: The play used to return the ball to the court from outside the baseline along the opponent's basket.

Baseline screen: A screen set near the *blocks* along the *baseline*.

Basket cut: A *cut* toward the basket.

Bench: Refers to *substitutes* sitting on the *sideline*, as well as to the bench they sit on.

Block: (1) A violation in which a defender steps in front of a dribbler but is still moving when they collide. Also called a "blocking foul." (2) To tip or deflect a shooter's shot, altering its flight so the shot misses. (3) The small painted square on the floor next to the basket just outside the *lane*.

Block out: To make contact with an opposing player to establish rebounding position between the player and the ball. Also called *box out*.

Bonus: A team is "in the bonus" when it accumulates seven or more team fouls in a half, giving the other team a *free throw* on each subsequent foul. Also called being "over the limit."

Bounce pass: A pass that bounces once before reaching the receiver.

Box-and-one: A combination defense in which four defenders play *zone* in a box formation and the fifth defender guards one player *man-to-man*.

Box out: To make contact with an opposing player to establish rebounding position between the player and the ball. Also called *block out*.

Box set: A formation in which four players align themselves as the four corners of a box. Often used for *baseline out-of-bounds plays*.

Brick: A bad shot that clanks off the backboard or rim.

Bump the cutter: To step in the way of a cutter who is trying to *cut* to the ball for a pass.

Carrying the ball: A violation that occurs when a player dribbling the ball brings her hand underneath the ball and momentarily carries it. Also called "palming."

Center: (1) The position in which a player, usually the tallest player on the team, stays near the basket. Also called the "5." (2) The player who plays that position.

Center circle: The painted circle at midcourt used for the opening *jump ball*.

Charge: (1) A violation in which a player with the ball runs into a defender who is standing still. Also called a "charging foul." (2) To commit that violation.

Chest pass: A pass thrown from the passer's chest to a teammate's chest. It can be a one-handed or two-handed pass.

Combination defense: A defense that is part *man-to-man* and part *zone*. Also called a "junk defense."

Continuity play/offense: A sequence of player and ball movements that repeats until a scoring opportunity opens up.

Control dribble: A dribble maneuver in which the player keeps her body between the defender's body and the ball.

Court sense: A term describing a player who plays smart basketball.

Court vision: A term describing a player who sees and understands what all the other players on the court are doing. This usually leads to having *court sense*.

Crossover dribble: A dribbling maneuver in which a player dribbles the ball in front of his body so he can change the ball from one hand to the other.

Cross screen: A movement in which a player *cuts* across the *lane* to *screen* for a teammate.

Curl pass: A low, one-handed pass made by stepping around the defender's leg and extending the throwing arm. Also called a "hook pass."

Cut: (1) A sudden running movement to get open for a pass. (2) To make such a move. Also called "flash."

Dead ball: A stoppage of play called by the referee.

Dead-ball situation: Whenever the referee blows the whistle and play stops for a foul, a time-out, or the end of a quarter.

Defend the basket: To prevent the player closest to the basket from getting the ball and scoring an easy basket.

Defensive rebound: A *rebound* made off a missed shot at the basket a team is defending.

Defensive slide: The quick "step-slide" movement a defender makes when closely guarding the dribbler.

Defensive stance: The stance used to play defense (knees bent, feet wide, arms out). Also called an *open stance*.

Defensive stop: Gaining possession of the ball before the offensive team scores.

Delay offense: An offense used to take more time with each possession.

Denial defense: A defense in which a defender tries to prevent her man from receiving a pass.

Denial stance: The stance used to play denial defense (body low, knees bent, hand and foot in the passing lane).

Deny the ball: To prevent the offensive player from receiving a pass.

Diamond-and-one: A combination defense in which four defenders play zone in a diamond formation and the fifth defender guards a specific offensive player man-to-man.

Double down: To drop from the perimeter, leaving one's man or zone, to *double-team* a *low post* player.

Double dribble: A violation in which a player picks up her dribble and starts to dribble again. A common occurrence with young players.

Double-teaming: A defense in which two defenders guard the same offensive player at the same time.

Down screen: A play in which a player comes down from the perimeter or *high post* area to set a *screen* for a player in the *low post* area.

Dribble: (1) To advance the ball by bouncing it on the floor. (2) The bounce of the ball caused by a player pushing the ball downward.

Dribble penetration: Attacking the seams between the zones with the *dribble*.

Drive: To attack the basket by dribbling hard at it.

Drop step: A *low post* move in which an offensive player with his back to the basket swings one leg around the defender and uses it as a *pivot foot* to gain inside position.

Dunk: A shot in which the player jumps high and throws the ball down through the basket. Also called a "slam," a "jam," and a "slam-dunk."

Elbow: The corner made by the intersection of the *free throw line* and the *lane* line. Each lane area has two elbows.

End line: The line that marks the playing boundary at each end of the court. Also called the *baseline*.

Entry pass: The first pass that begins a play.

Face up: See *square up*.

Fake/fake-out move: A move used to shake off defenders and create just enough space for an offensive opportunity.

Fast break: A play in which a team gains possession of the ball (through a defensive *rebound*, *steal*, or made shot) and then pushes the ball toward the other basket as fast as possible, hoping to catch the other team off guard and score an easy shot.

Field goal: A 2-point or 3-point basket.

Fight over the screen: When a player sticks out her hips and torso and then steps over the wide-leg stance of the *screener*.

Filling the lanes: A *fast break* in which players from the offensive team run up the court in the right lane, the middle lane, and the left lane.

Flagrant foul: Excessive physical contact (punching, kicking, etc.).

Flash: See *cut*.

Forward: A position usually played by a tall, athletic player. A "small forward" or a "3" plays on the *wing*, and a *power forward* or a "4" plays in the *high* or *low post* area.

Foul: A violation of the rules.

Foul line: The line behind which a player stands to shoot a *foul shot*. Also called the *free throw line*.

Foul line extended: An imaginary line extending from the end of the *foul line* to the *sidelines*. Also called the *free throw line extended*.

Foul shot: An uncontested shot taken from the *foul line* as a result of a *foul*. Also called a *free throw*. A successful foul shot is worth 1 point.

Foul trouble: (1) Player foul trouble occurs when a player accumulates three or four fouls and is in danger of fouling out. (2) Team foul trouble occurs when a team accumulates seven or more team fouls in a half and is "in the bonus."

Free throw: An uncontested shot taken from the *free throw line* as a result of a *foul*. Also called a *foul shot*. A successful free throw is worth 1 point.

Free throw line: The line behind which a player stands to shoot a *free throw*. Also called the *foul line*.

Free throw line extended: An imaginary line extending from the end of the *free throw line* to the *sidelines*. Also called the *foul line extended*.

Front: To guard a player by standing directly in front of him and therefore between him and the ball.

Frontcourt: A team's offensive half of the court. The opposite of the *backcourt*. Also refers to a team's *center* and *forwards*.

Full-court press: A *man-to-man* or *zone defense* in which the defensive players guard the other team starting while the other team still has possession of the ball in the *backcourt* before crossing midcourt. Also called a "press."

Give-and-go: An offensive play in which the player with the ball passes *(gives)* to a teammate and cuts *(goes)* to the basket to receive a return pass. One of the game's basic plays.

Goaltending: A violation in which a defender touches a shot as it nears the basket in a downward flight.

Guard: (1) A position on the perimeter. The *point guard* or "1" brings the ball up the court and begins the offense. The *shooting guard* or "2" is usually the team's best outside shooter. (2) To defend an offensive player closely.

Half-court line: The line at the center of the court parallel to the *baselines* that divides the court in half. Also called the "midcourt line."

Half-court offense: An offense executed once the team advances into the *frontcourt*.

Hand-check: To make hand contact with a dribbler while guarding her.

Held ball: A situation in which two players hold the ball in their hands simultaneously, but neither can pull it away from the other. Also called a *jump ball*.

Help and recover: A defensive move in which a defender leaves his assigned player to guard a teammate's assigned player and then goes back to guard his own player.

Help side: The half of the court (if the court is divided lengthwise) that the ball is not on. Also called the *weak side*. The opposite of the *ball side*.

Hesitation move: A dribbling maneuver in which the dribbler hesitates, pretending to pick up his dribble, but suddenly continues to the basket. Also called a "stop-and-go dribble."

High post: The area around the *free throw line*.

Hook pass: See *curl pass*.

Hook shot: A one-hand shot taken with a sweeping, windmill motion.

Hoop: The basket or rim.

Hoops: Slang term for the game of basketball.

Hops: A term used to describe how high a player can jump, as in "Eileen has great hops."

Inbound: To pass the ball to a teammate on the court from out-of-bounds.

Inbounder: The player who inbounds the ball.

Inbounds pass: A pass made from out-of-bounds onto the court to resume play.

Inside-out dribble: An advanced dribbling move, a fake *crossover dribble*.

Intentional foul: A foul that occurs when a player makes illegal contact with an opposing player without intending to get the ball.

Isolation play: An offensive play designed to have a specific player attack the basket 1-on-1. Also called "iso play."

Jab-and-cross: A play in which the offensive player makes a *jab step* in one direction and then follows it by driving by the defender on the other side.

Jab-and-go: See *rocker step*.

Jab step: A short (6 to 8 inches) out-and-back step by an offensive player to see how the defender reacts.

Jump ball: A procedure used to begin a game. The referee tosses up the ball in the center circle between two opposing players, who jump up and try to tip it to a teammate. Also called the "opening tip."

Jump hook: A variation of the traditional *hook shot* in which the shooter takes the shot with both feet in the air.

Jump shot: A shot in which the shooter faces the basket and releases the ball after jumping into the air.

Jump stop: The action of coming to a complete stop, legs apart and knees bent, when dribbling or running; can be a one-foot or two-foot jump stop.

Junk defense: See *combination defense.*

Key: See *lane.*

Kick it out: When the player driving to the basket passes the ball to an open player for a *jump shot.*

Lane: The rectangular painted area between the *baseline,* the lane lines, and the *free throw line.* Also called the "paint."

Layup: A shot taken next to the basket in which the shooter extends his arm, lifts his same-side knee, and aims the ball at the upper corner of the painted square on the backboard.

Lob pass: A pass made over a defender's head.

Loose-ball foul: A foul committed when neither team has possession of the ball.

Low post: The area on one side of the basket around the *block.*

Low post play: Any play that involves a pass to a *post player* positioned within close range of the basket.

Man: The player a defender is assigned to guard. Also short for *man-to-man defense.*

Man-to-man defense: A team defense in which each defender guards a specific player or *man.* Also called "player-to-player defense."

Man-to-man offense: A team offense used against *man-to-man defenses.* Also called "man offense."

Midcourt line: See *half-court line.*

Mirror the ball: To follow the movement of the ball with your hands when closely guarding a player who is *pivoting.*

Moving pick: A violation that happens when a *screener* leans or moves after setting a *screen.*

Net: The cord lacing that hangs down from the rim.

Nonshooting foul: A foul committed against a player who is not in the act of shooting.

Nothing but net: An expression that means the shot swished through the basket without touching the rim.

Off-ball screen: A *screen* set on a defender guarding an offensive player who doesn't have the ball.

Offensive formation: Tells the players where they should be at the start of a play. Also called an "offensive set."

Offensive rebound: A *rebound* at the basket a team is attacking.

On-ball defense: Defense that occurs when a defender guards the player with the ball.

On-ball screen: A *screen* set on a defender guarding an offensive player who has the ball.

One-and-one: *Free throws* awarded to a team once its opponent has committed seven *personal fouls.* If the shooter's first free throw is successful, she shoots a second free throw.

One-guard front: A *zone defense* that has one defender at or near the top of the circle. Includes the 1-2-2 and 1-3-1 zone defenses.

Open stance: The stance used to play *help-side* defense (feet apart, body balanced, knees bent, arms out). Also called a *defensive stance*.

Outlet: (1) To pass the ball after a defensive *rebound* to start the *fast break*. (2) The player who stays in the *backcourt* to receive an *outlet pass*.

Outlet pass: A pass made by a player on the defensive end of the court.

Overcommit: Occurs when a defender prematurely jumps into the air to defend what he thinks will be a shot.

Overhead pass: A two-handed pass thrown from above the player's head.

Overplaying: Playing very close and aggressively denying the ball.

Overtime: A 5-minute extra period played when the game is tied at the end of regulation play.

Paint: See *lane*.

Palming: See *carrying*.

Pass fake: See *ball fake*.

Passing line: The straight line between the passer and the receiver, or between the ball and the basket.

Personal foul: A penalty assessed on a player who commits an illegal action.

Pick: See *screen*.

Pick-and-roll: A two-person play in which one offensive player sets a screen *(pick)* on the ball handler's defender and cuts *(rolls)* to the basket after the ball handler drives by the screen. Also call a "screen and roll." A common play in college and the pros.

Pick up the dribble: Stop dribbling altogether.

Pivot: The action when the player with the ball spins on one foot and steps with her other foot to protect the ball from a defender.

Pivot area: See *high post*.

Pivot foot: The foot that the offensive player spins on while pivoting.

Player-control foul: A nonshooting offensive foul.

Player screen: See *off-ball screen*.

Player-to-player defense: See *man-to-man defense*.

Point guard: (1) A position played by a team's primary ball handler, the player who brings the ball up the court and begins the offense. Also called the "1." (2) The player who plays that position.

Pop out: A move in which a player moves *(pops)* to the *pivot*, *high post*, or *wing* areas.

Post: (1) A player who plays in and around the *lane* area. A *forward* or a *center* (a "4" or a "5"). (2) An area of the court, as in the *low post* or the *high post*.

Post up: (1) An offensive move in which an offensive player (usually a *forward* or a *center*) positions herself close to the basket with her back toward the basket and the defender behind her so the offensive player can receive a pass. (2) To make that move.

Power forward: (1) A position played by the larger of the *forwards* on the floor, usually a good scorer and rebounder. Also called the "4." (2) The player who plays that position.

Power layup: A two-footed *layup*.

Press: (1) See *full-court press*. (2) To engage in a full-court press.

Press break: A team offense used against a press defense. Also called "press offense."

Press offense: See *press break*.

Pressure defense: Aggressive defense to impede the progress of the ball up the court.

Primary break: A *fast break* that involves only a few players from each team.

Pump fake: A movement in which the player with the ball acts as if he's about to shoot. It is designed to trick the defender into straightening up, allowing the player with the ball to dribble past him. Also called a *shot fake*.

Push pass: A one-handed *air pass*.

Putback shot: A shot taken more or less promptly after the offensive *rebound* of a missed shot.

Quick hitter: A set play used to get the ball quickly to your best player so that she can score.

Quicks: A slang term used to describe how quick a player is, as in "Darnelle has average quicks."

Rebound: (1) A missed shot that comes off the backboard or rim. (2) To fight for and gain control of a missed shot that comes off the backboard or rim.

Recoil: When a player pulls back his jab foot.

Rejection: A blocked shot.

Reserves: See *substitute*.

Retreat step: A step in which the defender's back foot steps back as the offensive player moves forward, and the lead foot slides in place.

Rocker step: A play in which the offensive player makes a *jab step* in one direction and then follows it by driving by the defender in that direction. Also called the "jab-and-go."

Runner: A shot that a player shoots while running, without taking the time to set up the shot. Also called a "floater."

Safety: The offensive player at the top of the circle.

Sag/sag off: A tactic in which a defender leaves his *man* or *zone* and drops into the *lane* to help protect the basket.

Scissor play: A more advanced play that involves two *screen cutters* splitting the *high post* on both sides.

Screen: A play in which an offensive player runs over and stands in a stationary position next to a teammate's defender to free up the teammate to dribble or to receive a pass. Also called a "pick."

Screen away: To pass in one direction and set a *screen* for a teammate in the opposite direction.

Screen cutter: The player who uses a *screen* set for him by cutting shoulder to shoulder with the *screener*.

Screener: A player who sets a *screen*.

Seal off: When an offensive player blocks a defender from getting to the ball.

Secondary break: A *fast break* that involves most of the players from each team.

Set play: A sequence of player and ball movements that has an end.

Shooting foul: A violation that happens when a defender fouls the shooter.

Shooting guard: (1) A position played by a perimeter player who is usually the team's best outside shooter. Also called the "2." (2) The player who plays that position.

Shot clock: The clock used to limit the time allowed to attempt a shot. Shot clocks are used in pro and college games, but not in middle school and youth league games.

Shot clock violation: A violation that occurs when the team with the ball doesn't get a shot off during the allotted time. It results in a change of possession.

Shot fake: A movement in which the player with the ball acts as if she's about to shoot. It is designed to trick the defender into straightening up, allowing the player with the ball to dribble past her. Also called a *pump fake*.

Sideline: The line at each side of the court that marks the boundary of the playing surface.

Sideline play: A play used by the offensive team to put the ball back in play from the *sideline*.

Sixth man: The first *substitute* that comes off the *bench* to replace a starter.

Skip pass: An *overhead pass* from one side of the court to the other over the defense.

Small forward: (1) A position played by the smaller of the *forwards* on the floor. Also called the "3." (2) The player who plays that position.

Soft hands: A term used to describe a player who has good hand control with the ball; that is, who is a good passer and receiver.

Speed dribble: A dribble maneuver in which the player pushes the ball ahead of her and bounces it at chest height.

Spin dribble: A dribbling maneuver in which the player does a reverse *pivot* while bringing the ball around her so it ends up in her other hand.

Square up: To pivot so the shoulders and feet face the basket. Also called "face up."

Steal: (1) To intercept a pass and gain possession of the ball. (2) The name for the action.

Stop-and-go dribble: See *hesitation move*.

Stop and pop: An offensive move in which a player comes to a sudden stop, picks up her dribble, and shoots the ball.

Strong side: See *ball side*. The opposite of *weak side*.

Substitute: A player who comes in the game to replace another player. Also called a "sub."

Swing step: A step in which a defender makes a reverse *pivot* by swinging her lead foot behind the back foot.

Switch: A movement in which two defenders change the offensive player each is guarding.

Take it to the hole: Drive to the basket.

Technical foul: A violation, such as a player or coach using profanity, that results in the other team getting free throws and possession of the ball. Also called a "T," as in "T him up."

10-second call: A violation that occurs when a team is unable to advance the ball over the midcourt line before 10 seconds have elapsed.

3-point arc: A line drawn on the court 19 feet, 19 inches from the basket. Field goals scored from outside the arc count 3 points. Also called "3-point line."

3-point line: See *3-point arc*.

3-point shot: A shot taken from outside the *3-point arc*.

3 points the old-fashioned way: Scoring 3 points by making a 2-point shot, being fouled in the process, and making the *free throw*.

3-second call: A violation that occurs when an offensive player remains in the *lane* for 3 or more seconds.

Trailer: An offensive player, usually a *center* or a *power forward*, who trails the first wave of players on the *fast break*.

Transition: A movement that occurs when a team changes from offense to defense ("defensive transition") or from defense to offense ("offensive transition").

Trap: A defensive move in which two defenders guard the player with the ball by forming a V with their bodies.

Traveling: A violation that occurs when the player with the ball takes too many steps without dribbling. This is a common occurrence with young players.

Triangle-and-two: A combination defense in which three defenders play *zone* in a triangle formation and two defenders guard specific players *man-to-man*.

Triple threat position: The bent-knees stance that allows the player three options: dribble, pass, or shoot.

Turnover: A loss of possession of the ball caused by a *steal*, an offensive *foul*, or a poor pass.

Two-guard front: A *zone defense* that has two players (usually *guards*) at the top. Includes 2-3 and 2-1-2 zone defenses.

Two-guard offense: A team offense used against zones with one-guard fronts (1-2-2 and 1-3-1).

Two-shot foul: A violation that occurs when a defender fouls the shooter, and the shot misses. The shooter is awarded two *free throws*.

Up screen: An offensive play in which a player comes from the *low post* area to set a *screen* for a player in the *high post* area.

V-cut: An offensive play in which a player on the perimeter steps toward the basket, drawing the defender with him, and suddenly *cuts* to the perimeter for a pass. The opposite of a *backdoor cut*.

Walk up the line: Force the defender farther from the basket.

Weak side: The half of the court (if the court is divided lengthwise) that the ball is not on. Also called the *help side*. The opposite of the *ball side*.

Weak-side help defense: Help to the side of the court the ball is not on.

Wing: (1) The area on the court where the *3-point arc* meets the *free throw line extended*. (2) The offensive player who plays in that area.

Zone defense: A team defense in which players are assigned to guard specific areas (or "zones") of the court.

Zone offense: A team offense used against a *zone defense*.

Index

Acknowledgments

We would like to thank the following coaches for reviewing and providing helpful comments on the manuscript:

Josh Marko, Fairfield Ludlowe H.S., Boys' Basketball Head Coach, and PJ Wax III, Fairfield Ludlowe H.S., Girls' Basketball Head Coach.

Thank you also to the consummate professionals at McGraw-Hill, including Jon Eaton and Molly Mulhern, and Shelley Cryan Photography, LLC, for a terrific photo shoot. Kudos for a job well done to the youth athletes on our *Great Basketball Plays* demonstration team. Special thanks to the coaches and staff of the Temple University men's basketball team for helping our basketball photo shoot run smoothly. It's been a pleasure to work with all of you. Thanks also to Coach Joseph Signorile of Tomlinson Middle School (CT) for allowing Lawrence to sit in during practices, which gave him valuable insights into the strategy of youth basketball.

Lawrence would also like to thank Coach Richard O'Connell, who invited Lawrence to transfer to Rutgers Preparatory High School and play on his basketball team after Lawrence had been cut from the local Hillsborough High School varsity the year before, a seminal moment in Lawrence's life. He would also like to thank his eventual Hillsborough varsity coach, Jerome Leonardi. Both men instilled in Lawrence a love of the game, and the life lesson of clawing back despite setbacks.

About the Authors

Fran Dunphy is head coach of the Temple University men's basketball program, which he guided to back-to-back 20-win seasons, Atlantic 10 Conference championships, and NCAA tourney bids in 2008 and 2009. He was named 2008 Eastern College Coach of the Year. Prior to 2006 he was head coach of the University of Pennsylvania men's team, compiling a 310–163 record, nine 20-win seasons, and 10 Ivy League championships in 17 years.

Lawrence Hsieh is a writer and corporate attorney. He is a graduate of the University of Chicago Law School and Cornell University. He attended Hillsborough High School (NJ), where he was valedictorian and earned a varsity letter in basketball. He volunteers his time as a youth sports coach.